MAGIC IN ROMAN BRITAIN

ADAM PARKER

AMBERLEY

I dedicate this book to Katherine for helping to make this happen, and also to Orla for not helping it at all

First published 2025

Amberley Publishing
The Hill, Stroud,
Gloucestershire, GL5 4EP

www.amberley-books.com

ISBN: 978 1 3981 2081 5 (print)
ISBN: 978 1 3981 2082 2 (ebook)

British Library Cataloguing in Publication Data.
A catalogue record for this book is available from the British Library.

Typeset in 10pt on 13pt Celeste.
Typesetting by SJmagic DESIGN SERVICES, India.
Printed in the UK.

Appointed GPSR EU Representative: Easy Access System Europe Oü, 16879218
Address: Mustamäe tee 50, 10621, Tallinn, Estonia
Contact Details: gpsr.requests@easproject.com, +358 40 500 3575

Contents

Preface

I first became interested in the study of magic in the ancient world as an undergraduate at the University of Leicester in the late 2000s. It has been a research passion of mine ever since and became the subject of my Master's thesis, a series of scholarly articles in journals and edited volumes and culminated in my recently completed PhD thesis at the Open University. The content of this book is informed by the results of that PhD research. There is a problem within the study of ancient magic that introductions to the topic are bogged down in theoretical positioning and often take a broad-brush approach to the ancient world. This book will cut through these issues and so I hope that this will make the subject of ancient magic accessible to new audiences.

I must acknowledge the help and support of some excellent people. Firstly, thanks are always due to my PhD supervisors Helen King, Emma-Jayne Graham, and Ursula Rothe for guiding my project from its beginning to its end. More broadly, I am grateful for the support of the Open University Department of Classical Studies for supporting my PhD research intellectually as well as financially through the award of a research studentship grant. I am immensely grateful for all the helpful correspondence with museum curators around the country who helped me find magical objects hidden away in museum collections, and to the various unofficial members of the 'loony fringe' of Roman archaeology for their ideas, passion, and support.

Thanks for permission to freely reproduce certain images go to Andrew Parkin (Great North Museum), Dave Fell (Ecus Ltd), and Dawn Heywood (Lincoln Museum). Note that any image with a code starting 'PAS' in the caption (e.g. PAS: KENT-DD7BC3) has been produced and released by the Portable Antiquities Scheme. For their database see: www.finds.org.uk.

Latin words and phrases appear in the text in italics when within a sentence, though some will be in capital letters because they mostly refer to inscriptions which only used this case. The other conventions for writing Latin text are that if a word or words are missing, they are shown using an ellipsis (...) but if only a few letters are missing and they can be assumed or reconstructed then they are included in square brackets. For example, *ROMA[NI]TAS*. All Latin words will be translated into English where necessary. Additionally, place names outside of modern Great Britain will include an abbreviation of the country being referred to in parentheses.

Roman magic is my research passion, and it is a privilege to be able to share this research with all of you in this book.

1

Introduction

In the fourth century AD, in the bustling Romano-British town of Colchester, an infant died tragically young. They were buried in a coffin with a unique group of objects: a pierced tooth, a miniature phallic pendant, an amber carving depicting someone of African descent, a copper-alloy bell, two pierced coins, and a third coin held in a silver frame. These were found together with a copper chain, used for suspending them together as a group. All of these objects were, individually, magical things designed to protect the infant from supernatural dangers and they were included in this grave to perform this function in the afterlife – to protect the infant for eternity. Their grouping together speaks of an understanding both of the meaning of these symbols in the ancient world and the materials used to create them. They were magical objects which aimed to bring about a change in the world and provide protection in life and beyond it.

We will come back to this group of objects at the end of the book, but for now suffice to say that this incredible collection of interesting artefacts is an excellent way to introduce what magic looked like in Roman Britain. The subject of ancient magic remains understudied, and with this book I intend to promote interest in it as well as the archaeological study of ancient amulets. The focus here is on the ancient world and the geographical and chronological focus of this work is Roman Britain, a province at the north-western edge of the Roman Empire. The provinces of the north-west are covered by the modern countries of France, Belgium, the Netherlands, Great Britain, and parts of Germany. Britain was at the furthest edges of it. Of course, I will draw on some pieces of evidence from other places like these but situating this book within the one province of Roman Britain within the Empire provides an opportunity for in-depth discussions about what the experience of magic was like in this specific place. This focus on the material culture of magic in one province was a novel approach in my PhD research and I have adopted it here because I believe it provides greater insight. Some other introductions to ancient magic adopt a thematic approach to the subject and take in a very broad timeframe, often seeking to introduce magic from classical Greece to the end of the Roman Empire (a period of around a thousand years). This approach has its merits, and I recommend some recent scholarly examples of it at the end (see Chapter 13), but they paint a picture with a broad brush. It is undeniable that many aspects of the practices described in this book have their roots in older cultures, but this is only one part of their history. Roman Britain provides a smaller time window of four centuries to gaze through. The focus on one Roman province in this book creates opportunities for seeking individual expressions of ancient magic through archaeological remains and so an understanding of the experience of magic as well as its historical progression.

What is Magic?

It is important to outline what I mean by the word 'magic'. In modern scholarship it is a contested term, with different schools of thought arguing that it can be described in different ways. One of the major scholarly splits is between those who see it as wholly part of ancient religion and those who see it as something which was separate. For clarity, I fit into the second part of this scale, but ultimately this is a discussion about words and ideas rather than practices. That said, I think it is important to define exactly what I mean by 'magic' here. Roman magic can be defined as: 'a group of practices which aim to draw on the power of supernatural creatures, deities or natural elements in order to provide a benefit to the user'.

This book is then an introduction to the subject of ancient magic by presenting the different ways that this idea can be found in the Roman archaeology of Britain. Most often this means individual objects which can be linked to ancient magic by several ways – sometimes the objects have writing on them which can be linked to ancient documents and spellbooks, sometimes they are similar to things described by ancient authors, and sometimes they appear in strange and unusual places archaeologically. We will explore these different ideas. Very often the magical objects discussed functioned as amulets.

What is an Amulet?

In British museum displays and archaeological interpretation the description of an object as an 'amulet' is commonplace. All amulets were not equal, though, and in the ancient world differing amulets worked in very different ways. In very simple terms an amulet is something which was used by people to prevent them from suffering the effects of supernatural harms. Examples of this protection are against poor health, financial troubles, and social worries. Some specific amulets aimed to protect from drowning, or scorpion stings, or menstrual pains. Amulets were used by humans and certainly intended to protect their bodies, but they were also used to protect their spaces and often specific places (like homes and businesses). Some places were thought to be supernaturally dangerous, like crossroads or cemeteries, and amulets could be important there. They were also used to protect livestock and animal companions.

Amulets could work by aiming to cure a known problem or could be used to try and prevent something bad from happening. For the most part they were explicit in what they were supposed to do and what harm they protected their user from, but we will also encounter a generic and non-specific protection offered by some amulets. The difference in these approaches in Roman Britain seems to recognise that there are problems which can be expected and some which might come as a nasty surprise. Amulets gave their

This object is a Roman amulet on display in an archaeology museum in Britain. The label identifies it as an amulet, which is true, but there can a lot more be said about it. (Stephanie Holton, CC BY-SA 2.0)

users positive effects, like a sort of supernatural shield, to prevent harm or they could be used as a sort of medicine to cure or banish an existing problem. 'Charm' and 'talisman' are synonyms with 'amulet' here. We will explore how they worked through specific case studies later on and these will highlight the important components of amulets: materials, images, words, gestures, connections, and context.

The Evil Eye

Before we go on to start investigating the amazing magical objects which have survived in the archaeological record there is another technical term which can also be defined. 'Amulet' is covered in the above, but 'apotropaic' refers to something which has a supernaturally beneficial effect. Most amulets were apotropaic; the word derives from the ancient Greek word *apotropaios*, which translates as 'averting evil'. Many ancient amulets aimed to protect their users from the sorts of harms which could be inflicted by the Evil

Eye. Think of the Eye as a sort of personification of bad luck. The Evil Eye was depicted in art as a disembodied, unblinking eye and its gaze was feared. The gaze could be caught by doing certain things, 'given' or cast by someone else, and also averted by certain actions. Amulets were one of the main methods of averting it.

The main way that the Evil Eye survives in ancient art is in a particular artistic trope: the 'all suffering Eye', in which the Evil Eye is shown surrounded by its enemies. Presumably it was too dangerous to show the Eye without these protections. The symbols that surround the Eye, like on the most famous depiction from a mosaic from Antioch (SYR), might be considered amuletic in this circumstance. In the Antioch example the Eye is being stabbed by a sword and trident, pecked by a corvid, held by a scorpion, and a snake, dog, centipede, and leopard are advancing on it. Nearby a macrophallic dwarf is playing an *aulos* or *tibia* whilst facing away. This is a powerful group of images surrounding the Eye and preventing it from causing harm and it is a type of image which can also be found in Roman Britain.

The sources we can draw upon to learn about magic in the Roman Empire are threefold. Firstly, there are the surviving texts of classical authors. These include Pliny the Elder's

The mosaic from the House of Evil Eye, from Antioch. In the Hatay Archaeology Museum. (Public domain)

Gold discoidal earring depicting the 'all-suffering Eye'. A central Evil Eye is surrounded by its enemies, including a phallus, weapons, and animals. From Norton, Buckland and Stone CP, Kent (PAS: KENT-DD7BC3). (Kent County Council, CC BY 2.0)

A similar gold earring shows the Evil Eye with a different group of protective images surrounding it. Clockwise from top are a winged horse or lion, phallus, crab, snake, scorpion, arrow, and a bow and arrow. From Keswick, Norfolk (PAS: NMS-B9A004). (Norfolk County Council, CC BY 2.0)

'The Natural History', the medical works of Galen and Soranus, and assorted later works. Historical biographers like Tacitus, Suetonius, and Dio Cassius also tangentially mention the concept of magic when it comes into some matter of historical intrigue or imperial policy. Secondly, there are contemporary (ancient) documentary sources which talk about magic, spells, and amulets. In particular here I am referring to the *Papyri Graecae Magicae* ('Greek Magical Papyri') which are a series of ancient spellbook fragments surviving on papyrus from Roman Egypt. The *PGM*, as it will be referred to, include instruction manuals on how to perform some magical rituals and detail the components required, the words to be spoken, the time and place to do them, etc. The magical papyri are a hugely important source for the study of ancient magic, but the critical caveat is that we have no evidence for their dissemination and use in the north-western provinces, so users were (probably) relying upon other forms of information like word of mouth or the services of a ritual specialist. Thirdly, and most importantly for Britain, are the objects themselves. In some cases they include inscriptions which helpfully explain what their function was, but the majority of magical objects were not inscribed.

It is important to highlight that the evidence for magic in Roman Britain does not include every expression of magic in the ancient world. The following are not included in this book because the evidence for them happening in Roman Britain is slight or absent. Necromancy for one; there are a few unusual burials (so-called 'deviant burials' which aren't necessarily the same thing) which might include magical or ritual elements for restraining the dead, but these practices are so poorly understood that there could be other explanations. Divination was also an ancient magical practice, but it is so closely linked

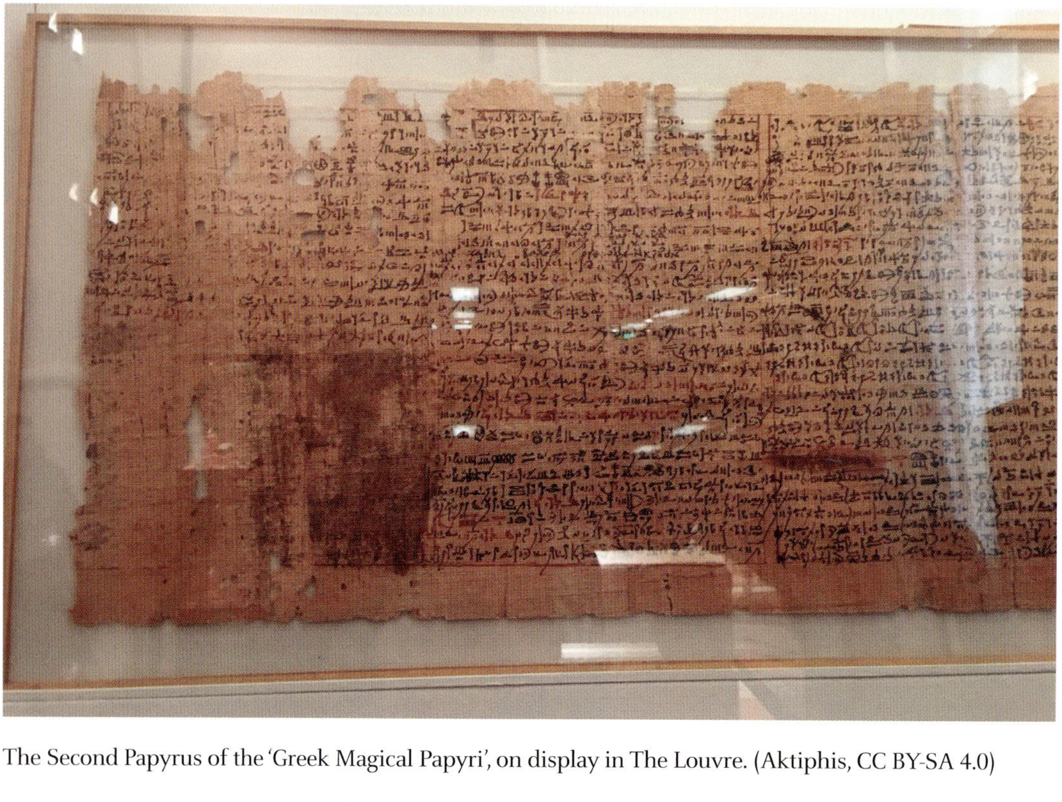

The Second Papyrus of the 'Greek Magical Papyri', on display in The Louvre. (Aktiphis, CC BY-SA 4.0)

A drawing of the god Set in the Greek Magical Papyrus XII.449-52. (Public domain)

to religious ritual activity it is difficult to disentangle and our understanding of it relies on surviving textual materials. There are also magical objects which are present elsewhere in the Roman world but not attested in Britain, including a possible magic wand and iron nails inscribed with magical symbols. With these caveats, this book now progresses to introduce the different expressions of magic in Roman Britain in their own chapters.

Unfortunately, not found in Roman Britain, these iron nails are inscribed with magical words and symbols. Different expressions of magic were found across the Roman Empire. (InsertClever, CC BY-SA 4.0)

2

Phallic Magic

Of all Roman amulets, phallic imagery is undoubtedly the one which is most familiar to the modern viewer. In media reporting of finds they are given a sensationalism which, as we will explore, misrepresents their true function.

Why Phalli?

Phalli may be considered amulets for several reasons. Most prominently is that they are shown in ancient art to be one of the enemies of the Evil Eye. They are shown as one of the attackers of the 'all-suffering Eye' amongst the other amulets. However, much more than any other amulet they are shown to be in direct conflict with the Eye in various ancient artistic media. This is especially true of carvings and mosaics. As a case in point, let's look at a carving from the ancient city of Leptis Magna (modern Libya): it depicts a large phallic beast (basically a phallus with legs and hooves) with a secondary phallus between its legs. This 'smaller' phallus is ejaculating over a disembodied Eye, which is also being attacked from above by a crab or

A relief of a carving in Leptis Magna (Libya) showing a phallus attacking the Evil Eye. (SashaCoachman, CC BY-SA 3.0)

scorpion. The crab/scorpion is a feature of the all-suffering Eye group, but here a double-phallus attack is the main focus of the relief. Ejaculating over the Eye was a crude way of trying to blind it – the blinded Eye would no longer be able to cast its gaze on the vulnerable and spread its malignant forces. The phallus versus Evil Eye narrative is a battle between good and evil, and through its depiction the phallus was always shown to be winning. These sorts of images, showing the narrative of the phallus defeating the Eye, can be found across the Roman Empire and are definitely present in Roman Britain. From this we learn that other images of phalli were also protecting people from evil and so this helps to explain the common use of phallic amulets.

Pendants, Mounts, Rings, Cups, and More

The commonest sorts of phallic object show a disembodied erect phallus, usually with testes. This necessity for the phallus to be erect was probably twofold: firstly, that it is only when erect that it could ejaculate and this was how it could attack the Evil Eye, and, secondly, that it is really very simple to create this shape. It required only a shaft and two rounded bits to be visually identifiable. So, in both two or three dimensions, phalli were easy to depict and this might have been beneficial to its popularity as an amulet.

That said, there was huge variation in the size and shape of these objects depending on what they were used for. Large pendants in copper alloys could measure over 5 cm and weigh more than 50 grams, whereas more delicate examples made from gold or silver weigh only a few grams.

Phallic pendants in copper alloy were incredibly popular personal adornments in Roman Britain. From Lyford, Oxfordshire (PAS: SUR-4DAF82). (Surrey County Council, CC BY 2.0)

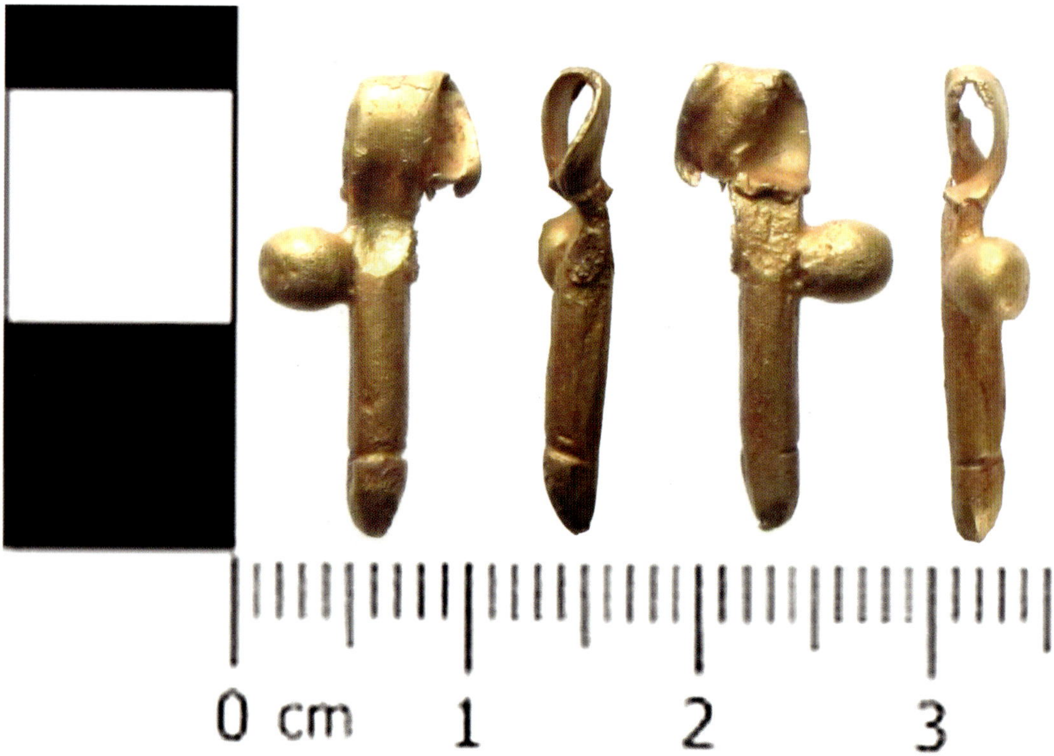

Above: Gold phallic pendant from Knaresborough, North Yorkshire (PAS: SWYOR-E56143). (West Yorkshire Archaeological Advisory Service, CC BY-SA 4.0)

Left: Gold finger ring with phallic decoration on the bezel. From Ayesbury Vale, Buckinghamshire (PAS: BUC-C9CEE4). (Portable Antiquities Scheme, CC BY 2.0)

Used for personal adornment, we find examples of phallic amulets in gold, silver, and copper alloy. Coppers were, by far and away, the most commonly used material. They were worn on the body in different ways. Around the neck they could be worn as a pendant, hanging from a simple thong or metal chain and resting somewhere between neck and chest. On gold finger rings they were delicately moulded; given the tiny gauges of these rings they were probably appropriate for children. They were used as belt mounts, toggles, and other forms of adornment. A specific type of phallic amulet unique to the north-western provinces was an antler burr (the cut end of a deer antler) upon which was carved a phallus (see also Chapter 10). Figurines as well as pendants could also be made more visually striking by adding wings, legs, or other body parts to the phallus. This links phalli, and probably the idea of sexual appetites, to wild animals and something out of control. In Roman art generally it was not unusual to see a disembodied phallus walking with a pair of hind legs which also had a mammalian phallus between them.

Phallic decoration was not only found on personal adornment, but also on more functional objects, like cups. Ceramic beakers made in colour-coated wares in the Nene Valley (mostly in Cambridgeshire) were decorated with applied clay motifs in a style called 'barbotine' and a type of this decorated them with phalli. Traditional decorations included floral patterns and vine swirls and the, much more famous, hunt scene. In the hunts, hares and deer are chased around the cup by hunting dogs. They were a very British design on a local product. Phallic decoration in this form does borrow from the traditional styles and, in some cases, adapts from them. Most famously is an example from Colchester in which a charioteer is driving a *quadriga* (four-horse chariot) pulled by phalli.The phallic decoration is quite unusual, even amongst the barbotine pattern forms. The phalli pulling the chariots are mimicking horses and others have designs with phalli which have wings and bird feet, linking the animal images on hunts to this particular style.

Some of the most sensational phallic objects, which can be downright bizarre to the modern viewer, were *tintinnabula* (phallic windchimes). The majority of examples are known from Pompeii and Herculaneum (IT), but a few in the north-western provinces attest to their use there as well. There is also one possible example from Colchester. *Tintinnabula* have a central figurine with a phallic element from which a series of chains were hung each carrying a bell. The figures were often phallic beasts – erect penises with legs and/or wings and sometimes with extra phalli as tails or between the legs. Unusual and fascinating objects, designed to move to touch or by wind power to create a jingling noise, *tintinnabula* were made to both catch the gaze of the Evil Eye and also to cause laughter. These objects probably appealed to the bawdy Roman sense of humour and the sound of laughter may have also been a way to dispel bad luck and supernatural evil.

Fist and Phallus

Another type of phallic amulet was joined to a different sort of amulet. In the Roman Empire, a clenched fist with the thumb protruding from beneath the forefinger was called the *manus fica* (also *mano fico*) which refers to the 'fig sign' (it literally translates as 'fig hand'). This was a real gesture made with human hands, and it was quite rude. The context is different but in terms of its rudeness it is loosely similar to the raised back of the middle finger in modern Western cultures. The fig sign may have been made with a pushing motion of the hand and arm towards its target, making a forceful, even penetrative, suggestion. It was used as an apotropaic gesture as well as an obscene one. Perhaps it was used because it was considered obscene and the Evil Eye could not bear to keep looking at it and would move elsewhere? The 'fig' is also an ancient literary pun linking it to female sexual parts, so there is a lot to unpack here.

The *manus fica* appears commonly on a dual amulet in which one side was a phallus and the other side was a hand making this gesture, referred to as 'fist-and-phallus' amulets. The fist and phallus are usually joined together by a plain shaft, which simply merged from phallus to wrist. The idea behind them is a sort of doubling of magical effects: a real-world protective gesture averting the Eye combined with the phallus, which aimed to do the same.

One important aspect of the fist-and-phallus amulets is that both parts would be clearly recognisable to a viewer as apotropaic things both individually and as a team.

Copper-alloy pendant or mount fragment with a hand making the *manus fica* gesture (PAS: KENT-4DA2EF). (Kent County Council, CC BY 2.0)

A group of six copper-alloy pendants from Catterick, North Yorkshire, depicting a phallus on one end and a hand making a *manus fica* variant on the other, each joined together by a scallop shell. There are three left and three right hands. In the Yorkshire Museum. (York Museums Trust (Yorkshire Museum), CC BY-SA 4.0)

Flaccid Phalli

Another lesser-known sort of phallic amulet depicted the male genitals in their flaccid state. These are infrequently found in the archaeological record. The earliest examples, from the first century BC in Europe, are carved in bone or ivory, but only copper-alloy examples have been found in Roman Britain. They show the phallus flaccid and usually resting on the testes, but sometimes slightly proud of them, which is different from the other phallic amulets discussed already. A particular point of difference is the inclusion of a triangular panel of pubic hair in these objects. Their function as amulets is largely pinned on their frequent use in connection with other amulets. Of nearly 500 phallic objects recorded from Roman Britain by the author, only thirteen were of this flaccid type, showing their relative rarity within the wider assemblage.

The association of flaccid phalli with an amuletic function might be called into question when one reviews the argument above for erect phalli used to fight the Evil Eye with their own bodily fluids. A flaccid phallus cannot ejaculate. It could urinate but this doesn't appear to be an artistic trope of a protective image. The linking of flaccid phalli to the same amuletic function as erect ones comes from the examples where they can be grouped with other well-known amulets.

In a popular type of harness pendant the flaccid phallus is central in the amulet but it also includes an erect phallus, the *manus fica* fist and a *lunula*, all of which are individually amulets. So it is through this association that we can argue that the flaccid phallus was an amulet. They are also found amongst some bigger assemblages of amulets from elsewhere in the Roman Empire.

Copper-alloy flaccid phallic pendant from Piercebridge, County Durham (PAS: BH-F31E4C). (Portable Antiquities Scheme, CC BY 2.0)

Tiny phallic decorations could decorate a wide range of clothing and straps. From Leafield, Oxfordshire (PAS: GLO-61A87A). (Bristol City Council, CC BY-SA 2.0)

Carvings Everywhere

Of all the phallic imagery from the Roman world, their depiction as carvings in stone might be the most familiar to a modern viewer. Such carvings are frequently points of interest to tourists who may find them *in situ* on monuments or in museums. Many people may also recall the modern received wisdom that 'phallic carvings pointed towards brothels'. It is important to highlight here, in no uncertain terms, that this was not the case. It is provably false. The idea seems to have been born out of a single example of a phallic carving on a street in Pompeii (located at the *Decumanus Maximus*); the incredible preservation of structures there allows one to draw a circumstantial relationship between this single carved phallus euphemistically 'pointing' towards the *lupanare* (the brothel). This ignores the many, many other phalli in Pompeii which did not point towards another building and the many hundreds around the Empire for which this is also true. It is also not how Roman advertising worked; they had no qualms about writing or drawing in explicit detail on public streets the names, skills, and prices of male and female prostitutes. There was no need for something quite so subtle in ancient Pompeii.

Like the other phallic objects, carvings were amulets but unlike jewellery and other objects they were not portable. Phallic carvings remained *in situ* on the building they appeared on until physically removed through destruction or repurpose. This is useful because it allows us to identify the sorts of places where they might be found archaeologically. There were two kinds of carvings: relief and inscribed. Relief carvings were cut with stonemason's tools and stood proud of the stone. These were primary stones included in the construction phase of a building. Incised carvings were probably added afterwards on an ad hoc basis and were scratched in by someone else. Both probably had equally magical properties, but they happened in different phases in the life of a building. From the archaeological evidence we find that carvings appeared at boundary places on walls, doors, and windows. In the Roman imagination these were liminal spaces and supernaturally dangerous places which needed extra protection.

Phallic carvings were sometimes joined by carved inscriptions. These are unusual but the examples from Roman Britain seem to use language which either highlights their magical function or was simply a bit crude. Some seem to be boastful about the size or owners of the phallus. An abbreviation *H P III* from Vindolanda translates as 'It is three feet long' and *VER / PAM / SEPT* inscribed on another from Maryport translates to 'The phallus of Marcus Septimius' and might be boastful or could intend to relate the amuletic protection to Marcus explicitly. The clearest magical or ritual links to inscriptions on phallic carvings from Westerwood which had *EX VOTO* inscribed. This phrase refers to the fulfilment of a vow to make the carving. The fragmentary inscription *[I]NVIDIO[S]IS MENTVLA*, probably from the fort at Netherby, north of Carlisle, translates to 'A phallic charm against the envious'. Referring to the earlier descriptions of the role the phallus played in deflecting the Evil Eye, the context of this inscription is very clear.

The most recent inscription from a phallic carving comes, again, from Vindolanda and was widely reported in 2022 because of the phrase *SECVNDIVS CACOR* carved on it as well. This translates as 'Secundius the shitter'! As ever there are different interpretations of this text. Perhaps it was an insult against Secundius? Or crude humour intended to embarrass him? It might be unlikely, but the carved phallus on the stone is very close, almost overlapping, so the text and could have been added afterwards to try and undo

A phallic carving on the floor of Chesters fort, on Hadrian's Wall. It is located within the *principia* (headquarters building). (CatfishJim, CC BY-SA 3.0)

The Evil Eye is being attacked by a phallus in this carving from Lincolnshire. It demonstrates the power of the image over bad luck. (Portable Antiquities Scheme, CC BY-SA 2.0)

the negative connotations it held. It is harder to argue that crude language added to the magical functionality of a phallic carving, but we should be mindful that if it was intended to be read not by people but by the Evil Eye then it might have also worked to fascinate, fix, and even mildly offend the Eye and so help to protect people from its gaze. There is also an argument that laughter could help dispel the negative power of the Eye, so this obscene phrase in an unusual place might have worked in this way. The interpretation of these sorts of images is very much in the eye of the beholder.

Vulvate Objects

As a mirror to this chapter, it is important to include the other sexual imagery used as amulets. Female genitals were also depicted on Roman objects, but in a more stylised form. The 'vulvate mounts' (sometimes unhelpfully called 'coffee-bean mounts') depicted a female pudendum as a raised oval boss with a longitudinal incision. They were cast in copper alloy. These mounts are associated with horse harnesses. Horses could be decorated with phallic amulets as well, and these were common, but this object type seems to be uniquely preferable for the protection of horses. It reveals something about the understanding of amulets in the ancient world: that there were certain types which were suitable for specific forms of protection and so there could be places where they might be expected. The presumption is that they also worked to fascinate the Evil Eye through being a rude image in an unusual place.

Over 150 examples of this object have been identified from Roman Britain and it is an object which has benefited greatly from the advent of metal detecting and the reporting of finds through the Portable Antiquities Scheme website. Compare this figure, though, to the more than 450 phallic objects. Is this a reliable number? Were phallic objects really three times more prominent than vulvate ones? It's difficult to tell using these broad numbers. One issue with the many detected finds of vulvate mounts is that they aren't then found with other objects which might help to date them, so we don't have a good sense of exactly when they became popular and if their popularity waned over the Romano-British period.

It is interesting to note that the vulvate forms of decoration are rather more subtle than the phallic imagery already presented. Partly this seems to be an issue of biology – a simple tube shape with two spheres might easily represent a phallus, but a disembodied vulva was, apparently, more complicated to represent in ancient art. The form of the mounts shown here is, in fact, one step removed as they were probably as likely to represent cowrie shells as human vulvas. This is because of the linking of these shapes in the ancient world and goes some way to explain the subtlety in their shapes.

Female sexual parts were also used as amulets on Baubo figurines. Baubo is a character from ancient Greek mythology and is sometimes considered as a personification of mirth, or at least of bawdy humour. Such figures are probably absent from Roman Britain, but highlight the use of clear, female, sexual imagery as an amuletic image. These show a human female, nude, in a deep squat and often with one hand between her legs separating her labia.

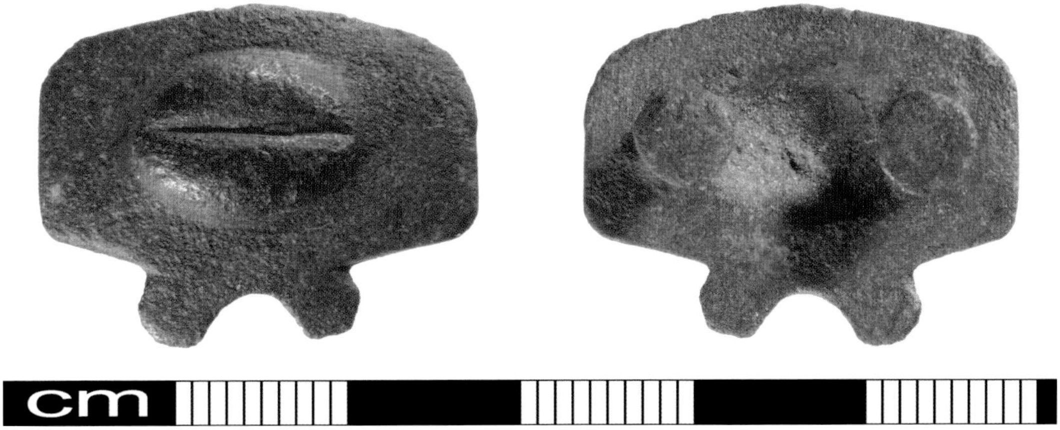

It was, perhaps, less obvious than the phallic images, but this oval shape depicts a stylised vulva and it was frequently used as decoration on copper-alloy mounts with a hexagonal-shaped backing. From Swaffham, Norfolk (PAS: NMS-735E56). (Norfolk County Council, CC BY-SA 4.0)

A complete vulvate mount with harness pendant. When on a horse harness the hanging object could move and might have created a metallic jangling sound. From London (PAS: LON-9A3504). (Portable Antiquities Scheme, CC BY-SA 2.0)

3

Magical Gemstones

Many types of metal finger rings worn in Roman Britain survive in the archaeological record and a great number of these were made to hold a semi-precious stone setting. Some stones were plain but carved designs were popular throughout the Roman period. Often these depicted a deity or an animal, but there were subtle connections between both the stones and the images which created powerful objects. We'll explore the simpler designs later on, but a true magical gemstone incorporated at least one image and some carved text, usually in Greek. They often had many visual designs added to them and were astonishingly complex images.

Welwyn Charm

The best example of this type in Britain is the Welwyn Charm, found at Dicket Mead in April 1963. It was found in a deposit dating to the fourth century. The oval ring setting is carved from haematite and measures 17mm × 13.5mm. On the front it has a carved figure of the goddess Isis (a Romano-Egyptian goddess) with the Egyptian deity Bes to one side and a lioness to the other. Beneath these characters are a uterine symbol (appearing as a globular pouch with tentacles beneath it) and a seven-toothed key facing upwards. Greek vowels are carved around these figures and all together they are surrounded by an Ouroboros symbol (a snake eating its own tail). On the outside of the snake, at the edge of the stone, is a thirty-letter Greek word. This word is nonsensical, so it doesn't translate to anything that we can understand, but it appears to be a palindrome – a word that reads the same backwards and forwards. The almost-palindrome is *Λ[E]MEINΛE[BΛRW]ΘEPEΘWPΛBEΛENIEMEΛ*, which transliterates to 'AEMEINAEBAROTHERETHORABEAENIEMEA'. Lots of these elements are, individually, magical symbols and we can hear about them from spells in the *PGM* as well as on magical gemstones from other places. All of this content is just the front. The back of the stone is also carved and has a scarab beetle (the sacred scarab, perhaps familiar from Egyptian history), another of the uterine symbols, and more unusual writing. The Greek text on this side is an example of a *vox magica* ('magical name'), a word which only appears to have had a magical function. The most familiar example of a Roman *vox magica* to a modern, English-speaking reader is probably *abracadabra*. Whilst this is traditionally used in entertainment and conjuring now, the word is first attested in a spell by Serenus Sammonicus to cure fever and dates from the second or third century AD. The *vox magica* on the back of the Welwyn Charm is *ΟΡWΡΙΟΥΘ ΙΛΗWΙΛWΛWΙ* ('ORORIOUTH IAHO IAO AOI'). This gemstone includes a significant amount of imagery and text and would have required a lot of arcane knowledge to understand. Given how small it is, it would have been very difficult for someone other than its wearer to see the images and text and be able to interpret them without very close proximity to the ring. This gemstone included a lot of the elements of ancient magical rituals: arcane words (the vowels and palindrome), supernatural powers (the deities), and special ingredients (haematite). In this example we interpret the gem as being a cure for a medical problem described in the ancient world as 'wandering womb'. This pseudo-medical condition was informed by an ancient understanding that the womb was not fixed in place within women's bodies but could become mobile, causing all manner of physiological and psychological problems. One other 'treatment' for it relied on the belief that the womb was attracted to pleasant scents and so could be coaxed back into place by the application of nice-smelling balms to intimate parts.

The complex magical imagery of the Welwyn gemstone includes deities, amuletic images, and arcane words.

The true magical gemstones are rather rare in Roman Britain, with fewer than ten examples, but the corpus of these objects from the wider Empire is recorded in the Campbell-Bonner Magical Gems Database (cbd.mfab.hu) which estimates the total number of known examples to be over 5,600. So, generally, they were popular objects. They also show incredible variations in style, size, and content. Many different deities, supernatural entities, and magical formulae were used to create bespoke amulets aimed to protect or cure specific problems.

The Magic of Gems

Simpler gemstones which contained only an engraving of one or several figures and did not include words or magical formulae were much more common in Roman Britain. Relationships between certain images and specific gemstones (especially the particular colours of gemstones) are apparent and corroborated by some ancient texts. The imagery on these gemstones might have intended to represent certain qualities and so bestow or enhance these in the person who wore them. This is the magical idea of *similia similibus curantur* ('like cures like'). It was a complicated idea with a broad application, but the theory goes that similarities could be powerful. With gemstone carvings the depiction of a scorpion, for example, may have been used to protect against scorpion stings. The threat of scorpion stings in ancient Britain was not very high at all (there are no native scorpion species in the British Isles) but the example is common enough in the Mediterranean provinces. The scorpion gems were usually carved into yellow jasper.

In Britain there are thousands of gemstones (also called 'intaglios') from Roman sites and not all of these served a magical or amuletic function. There are many different deities depicted on gemstones which may have aimed to imbue or embody certain qualities in a similar sort of way. In a study by Dr Ian Marshman of all carved Roman gems in Britain he found that the god Bonus Eventus was the most commonly depicted. Bonus Eventus is a male consort of the goddess Fortuna (the goddess of fortune) and his name translates as 'good outcomes'; so he was the personification of good luck. Good luck is a quality very similar to the supposed effects of amulets - a supernatural benefit which aims to provide positive things to the user. Clearly they were allied.

A red carnelian intaglio (originally set into a ring) depicting a male figure holding two ears of corn and a lagobolon holding a snared hare over one shoulder. This is Bonus Eventus, the personification of good luck and good outcomes. Wearing a ring to this god was supposed to help bring good fortune. From Thornbury, Gloucestershire (PAS: GLO-EB93D3). (Bristol City Council, CC BY-SA 4.0)

Powerful Gods

Wearing an image of a deity on a ring showed respect of, and allegiance to, their powers. The qualities of deities are well known (for instance Mars, the god of war, and Venus, goddess of love) but other gemstones depicted certain unusual scenes which might have been more arcane. Images of Hercules fighting the Nemean Lion in one of his mythical labours were common and were probably also linked to other images of a 'victorious lion' where the lion has made a fresh kill. The Hercules gems often included a carving of his club, but he was rarely holding it, and it was instead shown as floating off to one side. Hercules clubs were separately worn as amulets. Hercules versus the lion probably embodied several ideas, including physical strength, personal victory, and overcoming adversity.

Certain supernatural entities, probably less familiar to modern readers than Hercules, were also depicted on gems to provide specific protections. The lion-headed serpent creature called Chnoubis is one such figure. It usually wore a radiating crown of light and could particularly be found carved on green stones to protect from stomach complaints. Another unusual character, Abraxas, was particularly favoured for gemstones. Abraxas had the body of a man, head of a cockerel, and snakes for legs. It carried a whip in one hand, a small shield in the other, and was often accompanied by Greek letters IAW ('IAO'). These sorts of carved gems were intended to provide a specific sort of magical or medicinal effect, but we can't always be sure about what this was. This is also true of two classes of

Above left: A gemstone carved with the figure of Abraxas – a Gnostic deity with a cockerel head and snake legs. He carries a whip in one hand and a shield in the other. Several similar examples have been found in Britain. In Thorvaldsens Museum. (Public domain)

Above right: The Gnostic deity Abraxas shown in an impression from a magical gemstone. In the University of Tartu Art Museum, Estonia. (Tartu Art Museum via Europeana, CC BY-ND 4.0)

Above left: Gemstone set within its original ring. Magical gemstones were designed to be worn on rings of iron, copper, silver, or gold. The gem here depicts the goddess Diana. This ring could also have been used as form of amulet. Diana was closely associated with young girls, hunting, and ideas of protection (PAS: NMS-90F486). (Norfolk County Council, CC BY 2.0)

Above right: Rarely, finger rings included magical words inscribed into the metal and not a gemstone. The SSS device is associated with Chnoubis on other magical gemstones and was probably another way of invoking the protective healing powers of the deity. From Sporle with Palgrave, Norfolk (PAS: LVPL-22C604). (National Museums Liverpool, CC BY-SA 4.0)

particularly unusual carvings showing either a bearded man which had another human or animal at the back of its head called 'Grylloi', and seashells which had animals emerging from them. The bearded man sometimes had a youthful face merging with his which became visible when turned upside down but he was also joined to exotic animals. Grylloi might have invoked ideas of youthfulness or the idea of time and the life course.

Other gemstones might have provided some sort of magical effect simply due to the strangeness of their carvings. Unusual, uncommon, arcane knowledge is a part of ancient magical practices though we must be careful to avoid assuming in the modern world that everything that we don't understand from the ancient one had a supernatural effect or ritual function.

Collyrium Stamps

There are a number of carved stone stamps, all small and usually rectangular, called *collyrium* stamps or 'oculists stamps' and these included a Greek or Latin phrase inscribed backwards – when stamped, the text could be read normally.

What is interesting is that the stamps were intended to be medicinal and the texts refer to certain medications. A good example of this is the one from York. In two backwards-carved lines it reads: 'IVLIALXANDRI / DIAMYADASP', 'Julius Alexander's salve made from misy for aspritudo'. Aspritudo was a description of an eye condition where the symptom was roughness or graininess. Misy probably refers to copper pyrite and was included here as a medicinal ingredient. In Wroxeter, another example includes details of how to use it: 'L. IVL SALVTARIS PE / NICILLUM AD LIPPUD', 'Lucius Julius Salutaris's salve to be applied with a brush for the lippitudo (of the eyes)'. Lippitudino refers to an inflammation of the eyes. A square stamp from Kenchester has the name of the healer Titus Vindacius Ariovistus inscribed and then, on each long edge, a different named preparation. It has stamps for 'nard-oil salve', 'green-salve', 'infallible salve', and 'frankincense salve'.

Whatever concoction the oculists' stamp was pressed into was given as a medication for eye conditions. It is likely that it was some sort of paste, formed into a pill, containing the ingredient advertised. The *collyrium* stamps often included decoration or carvings which were very similar to those on magical gemstones. The carvings on gemstones were also written backwards and many of them could have functioned as stamps as well as worn objects. In the examples with Greek text, which was read normally, like the Welwyn Charm, these were probably not used for stamps because the resulting stamped text would be backwards. It is an intriguing idea, entirely without evidence in Britain, that some magical gems were stamped onto other materials in order to bestow a magical effect upon them. Or perhaps the stamps added a level of authenticity for their creator that their preparations were reassuringly created by someone with access to arcane knowledge. They might have been medicines, like salves, pastes and pills, but many other organic materials could be stamped and so we should remain open-minded to the possibilities of their use.

A *collyrium* stamp from York marked, in retrograde, with the name of Julius Alexander and his products. (York Museums Trust (Yorkshire Museum), CC BY-SA 4.0)

4

Lamellae and Amulet Cases

Gold was a valuable resource in Roman Britain and was available only to the wealthy. There was a gold coin in circulation during the early Imperial period, called an *aureus,* which was worth twenty-five times the value of the nearest coin, a silver *denarius.* At the end of the first century AD, a Roman legionary was paid 300 *denarii* a year. Theoretically they could be paid their yearly wages in 12 of the gold *aureii.* This was incredibly unlikely to ever happen, but it goes to show the high value of gold as a resource.

Gold was used for all sorts of personal adornment, especially earrings, finger rings, and beads. A special sort of amulet called a *lamella* was also used in the ancient world and eight *lamellae* have been found in Roman Britain. A *lamella* was a thin gold sheet, usually a few centimetres in length, upon which magical formulae and spells were written. Usually they were thin, narrow strips in a rectangular shape. Translations of the text clearly identify the purpose of most amulets and the sorts of harms they were designed to protect against. The finished texts were rolled up and placed within small, cylindrical, gold containers, now commonly called 'amulet cases'. Elsewhere in the Roman Empire the amulet cases could be made of copper alloy or silver instead of gold but all of the British examples we know about have been made of gold.

We can link *lamellae* and amulet cases as part of the same amulet practice because of examples found across Europe where the rolled-up *lamellae* have been found inside one of these cylindrical cases. The amulet cases have suspension loops on one side, showing that they were supposed to be strung and used like jewellery. Slightly confusing this link are the examples where amulet cases were still sealed but found to contain things other than *lamellae.* Examples in the British Museum contained powdered sulphur as a sort of magical substance held within the amulet case instead of a *lamella.*

Fabia's Charm

A *lamella* found in Oxfordshire in 2007 tells a particularly interesting story. Although it is only a small and thin rectangle of gold sheet measuring 63 × 28mm and weighing 1.4g, it was inscribed across sixteen lines. The first three lines are all *charaktêres* ('characters')

A gold *lamella* protecting Terentia during childbirth. From Oxfordshire (PAS: BERK-0B6771). (Portable Antiquities Scheme, CC BY-SA 4.0)

which are nonsensical symbols that look a bit like letters. These are common in ancient magical formulae. The remaining thirteen lines are all written in Greek handwriting. The translation identifies that the function of the amulet was to protect a woman called Fabia, daughter of Terentia, through childbirth. In full, the text reads: 'Make with your holy names that Fabia whom Terentia her mother bore, being in full fitness and health, shall master the unborn child and bring it to birth; the name of the Lord and Great God being everlasting.' It's important to note that the 'Lord and Great God' is not the Judeo-Christian God. This phrase appears in many other amulets from the Roman Empire and from these we learn that it is referring to a different supernatural power. The gold leaf and its text was rolled up and most likely worn by Fabia herself in an amulet case during pregnancy and labour to ensure a safe birth. What is fascinating about this inscription is that it gives us a rare insight into the specific circumstances where the amulet was supposed to work. Labour and birth is a process which could take hours or over a day, but it identifies that Fabia's *lamella* was not something which she wore everyday of her life. It was a time-limited device with a specific function in mind. Perhaps it was worn for the weeks or months before childbirth to start the protection early or to store up some power for the big day. This is a significant difference to other sorts of amulets because we often think of them as being worn by people for a much longer period. Often there are discussions about amulets which were supposed to be used generally by children and adults, or by men or women. Fabia's amulet shows that using magical objects could be a very bespoke, focussed, and time-limited practice.

Gold amulet case from the Church Street sewer, York. (York Museums Trust (Yorkshire Museum), CC BY-SA 4.0)

Amulet case from Pondesbury, Shropshire (PAS: HESH-5D3DF6). (Portable Antiquities Scheme, CC BY 2.0)

Tiberius' Charm

An example of a *lamella* from Billingford (Norfolk) was also inscribed in Greek (on a thin gold leaf 41mm × 30mm) and reads: 'Iao, Abraxas ... ablannathanalba give health and victory [to] Tiberius Claudius Similis whom Herennia Marcellina bore'. Health and victory are two important concepts in the ancient world. There is a temptation to think of Tiberius as a soldier or a gladiator who may be in dire need of both of these qualities, but the reality is that this could be an appropriate charm for a large portion of Romano-British society. Ancient magical spells like this did often rely on matronymics (the names of mothers) as part of their power. Hence Tiberius was named as the son of Herennia Marcellina and Fabia named as the daughter of Terentia. Another magical device in this charm is the use of strange words. It has an almost-palindrome, so almost reads the same forwards and backwards. In Greek lettering ablannathanalba is: αβλανναθαναλβα. The extra letter *nu* may have been a mistake. Unusual and nonsensical words like palindromes were added to enhance the magical power of the amulet. It also had some *charaktêres* drawn around the edge of the amulet.

Powerful deities and magical words were invoked in this gold *lamella* to protect Tiberius Claudius Similis. From Billingsford, Norfolk (PAS: NMS-7BEED8). (British Museum, CC BY-SA 4.0)

Gold and Lead

Pliny the Elder (HN 33.25) hints at a Roman understanding that gold had more value than its mundane, economic one: 'gold is efficacious as a remedy in many ways, being applied to wounded persons and to infants, to render any malpractices of sorcery comparatively innocuous that may be directed against them'. The colour of gold was also linked to solar deities in the ancient world because of its allusion to the colour of the sun and so we get this sense that gold was inherently powerful. In part this might also be linked to its important social function because it was an exotic, desirable thing for special magical purposes as well as economic ones. In the ancient world there were also certain laws which prevented citizens from wearing specific colours, clothes, or jewellery without the appropriate social status. The men of the middling rank of Roman society, the *eques*, were identified by the gold ring they could wear on a finger. Fabia's amulet was designed to be worn for a relatively short period of time and then, presumably, not used again in the same way so it was a single use of expensive gold. It is possible that this added to its magical potency.

Left: A fragmentary *lamella*, which had been rolled. The text is, unfortunately, illegible. From Kirk Smeaton, North Yorkshire (PAS: SWYOR-8F0C84). (British Museum, CC BY-SA 4.0)

Below: *Lamellae* were rolled before being folded into amulet cases. This example from Benniworth, Lincolnshire, remains rolled up. (Lincolnshire County Council, CC BY-SA 4.0)

An exceptionally well-preserved *lamella* that shows the repeating Greek characters and arcane symbols that enhanced its magical function. This amulet protected Aurelia from epileptic seizures. (Getty Museum, public domain)

A complication to this idea that gold was magically powerful is the use of a different metal, lead, for the same sorts of *lamellae*. There are four examples of lead *lamellae* from Roman Britain. They were generally much thicker than the gold examples, but the translations of their text show that they fulfilled the same sort of function. Lead will be discussed in much greater detail alongside curse tablets in Chapter 5. A lead *lamella* from West Deeping (Lincolnshire) was an amulet to protect from either a specific uterine problem or the ancient condition of a 'wandering womb': 'Womb, I say to you, stay in your place ... has given to you. I adjure you by Iao, and by Sabao and by Adonai, not to hold onto the side; but stay in your place, and not to hurt Cleumedes(?) daughter of A [...]'.

This text is fragmentary. Wandering womb was a so-called affliction noted by the Greek physician Hippocrates and discussed by many later ancient (and then medieval) authors. As mentioned already, the theory was that the womb was not affixed in a specific place in the body and when not being used during pregnancy could move around the body, causing trouble. The lead *lamella* above applies this 'medical knowledge' to their situation and calls on the powers of several supernatural figures – Iao, Sabao (usually Sabaoth), and Adonai – to fix it in place and prevent the patient, Cleumedes, from being in pain.

Lead sheet is a rare material to be inscribed with an amulet, as with this example from West Deeping, Lincolnshire. (© Lincolnshire County Council, Lincoln Museum)

5

Curses

There is significant evidence for the use of curse tablets in the north-western provinces and especially in Roman Britain, where several hundred examples have been recorded. The tablets are the results of a cursing ritual involving a user writing a grievance against another person (or group of people) and calling upon divine and dangerous powers to perform malevolent, physical things in retribution.

In the second century AD Docilianus dedicated a curse at the sacred spring at Bath, in the Temple of Sulis-Minerva. A translation of the text reads:

> Docilianus [son] of Brucerus to the most holy goddess Sulis. I curse him who has stolen my hooded cloak, whether man or woman, whether enslaved or free, so that the goddess Sulis should inflict the greatest death upon him and not allow him sleep or children now and in the future, until he has brought my hooded cloak to the temple of her divinity.

What is a Curse Tablet?

Curse tablets are sometimes called *defixiones* from the Latin verb *defixio* 'to nail down', referring to the act of driving nails through some finished curses. Docilianus' curse was pierced by a nail after it was written, presumably by its composer. Not all *defixiones* were actually nailed so 'curse tablet' is a more accurate description of this object type. In Britain they were made from small sheets of lead alloys and were usually rectangular in shape. Similar to the *lamellae* (Chapter 4), they were handwritten by someone scratching the letters into the metal with a sharp-pointed tool. A difference between *lamellae* and curses is that Latin and Celtic were the languages used in cursing rather than Greek. Illustrations of surviving curses may appear almost illegible to a modern viewer because we are so used to seeing ancient Latin writing in bold capital letters on tombstones, altars, and other dedications. Handwritten Latin looked quite different to the carved examples and curse tablets capture this well.

Writing a curse required the text to be scratched onto the surface of the lead using a stylus. For many of the people cursing they would be unfamiliar both with the act of handwriting in this way and scratching prose onto a metal surface.

Curses were usually scratched on lead sheets and sometimes were folded and then had nails driven through them to hammer home the point. Curses in Roman Britain were usually deposited at specialist ritual sites, so we find larger numbers of them at the Temple of Sulis-Minerva at Bath and the shrine to Mercury at Uley in Gloucestershire. Elsewhere in the Empire large numbers have been found at the Temple of Magner Mater at Mainz (DE) and cemeteries at Sousse and Carthage (TN). It is interesting to note that the practice continued later in Roman Britain than in these other places.

Curse from Ratcliffe on Soar, Nottinghamshire, cursing the theft of a mule. The text is shown in red lettering (PAS: LEIC-9874E9). (Derby Museums Trust, CC BY 2.0)

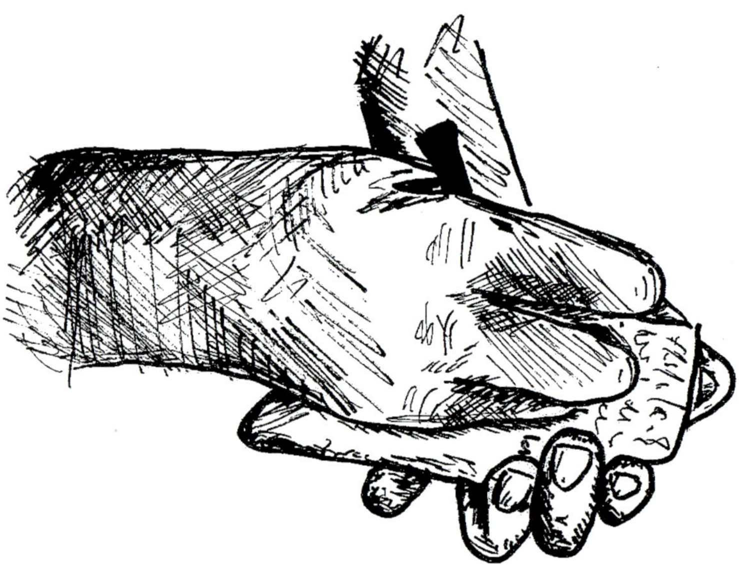

Making a curse could mean holding the metal plate and stylus in an unfamiliar way as this was an unusual way of making a written text. (Illustration by the author)

The Purpose of Cursing

Cursing was a process in Roman Britain. There were many different motivations for making a curse in the ancient world (to curse gladiators and charioteers, personal enemies, political rivals, and also unrequited lovers) but in Britain it was mainly used for condemning thieves. Cursers (the people making the curse) were almost always victims of theft. The contents of the theft were often included in the cursing text and so we can find out the range of property losses which could result in a curse.

From curses at Bath we find that Basilia had a silver ring stolen and Civilis had a ploughshare (an iron part of a plough) stolen. A curse from Pagan's Hill cursed Vassicillus for the theft of 3,000 *sestertii*, a huge amount of money. Relatively mundane losses could also result in curses. Docilianus, as we have seen, had a cloak stolen and another by Docimedis is for the loss of two gloves, cursing the thief with blindness. Although fairly low-value items, the loss was considered important to the victim. Sometimes the writing identifies that the curse stops if the grievance is resolved, for example, when a stolen item is returned. This is the case of the example given above, where Docilianus curses the thief '*until he has brought my hooded cloak to the temple*'. Presumably at this point the curse would be lifted automatically.

It is likely that the curse was enacted when other means of getting the property back were no longer available. There is a lot of research into the psychology of cursing and it is understood to have been both satisfying for the curser because they were able to do something to amend their poor situation and push back against the thief, but it could also be problematic for a thief if their victim was publicly known to have made a curse. A fear of the supernatural consequences of a curse could have, potentially, convinced a thief to return stolen property. The get-out clause which ended the curse is relevant for a thief who understands themself to be cursed. Although sometimes pierced with nails, curses were not nailed up somewhere on public display, and so a thief would not know if the power of the curse could be lifted. Some victims donated the stolen property to the god of the shrine where the curse was made as part of the cursing ritual. This changed the theft from not just a crime against a person but a sacrilegious act against the god. For example, Basilia's lost ring was presented, in text, to the god Mars and so the visceral punishment she called down on the thief was religiously justified.

> Basilia presents to the temple of Mars [her] silver ring. If enslaved or free man has been involved, or knows anything about it, he may be accursed in [his] blood and eyes and all his limbs, or even with all his intestines eaten away: he who has stolen the ring or was a witness is done for.

We don't know whether curses actively changed the behaviour of thieves in Roman Britain or if they acted as a general deterrent against crime, but through them we do learn a lot about the injustice of some parts of the ancient world as well as what individuals thought was important. The function of curses, which was to cause physical trauma to other people by supernatural means, is exactly the sort of thing that amulets intended to ward against.

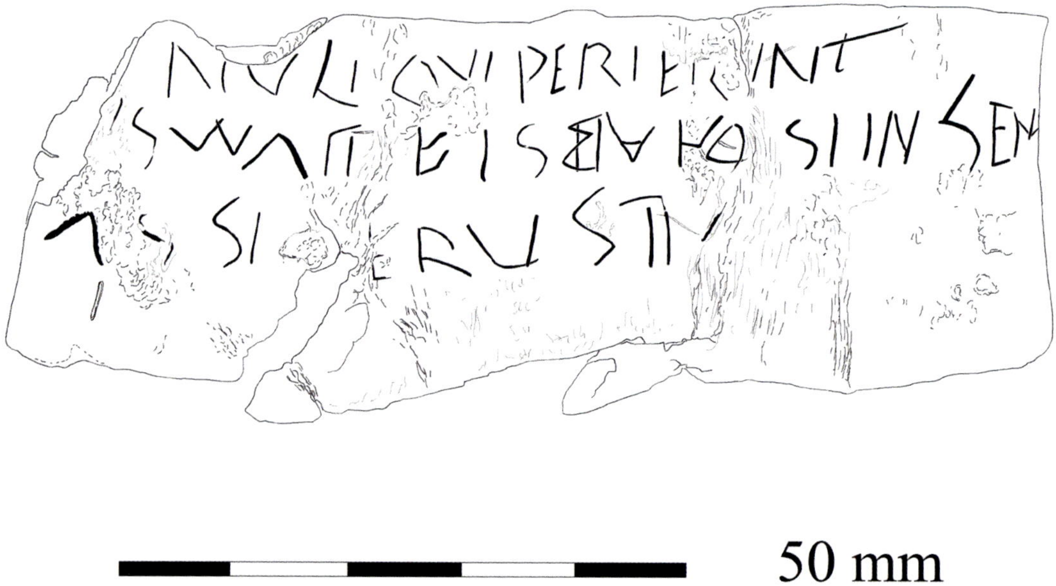

An illustration of a curse against someone for the theft of rings. The second line includes some additional magical elements with letters reversed or inverted to add extra power to the curse. From Lidgate (Suffolk) (PAS: SF-BA1337). (Suffolk County Council, CC BY 2.0)

After being written, some curses were folded and impaled with nails to show extra anger. The nails could be aimed to drive through the names of the people being cursed to attack them further. From London. (Public domain)

Cursing Places

Bath and Uley were important shrines where cursing was clearly part of their day-to-day function. We might think of them as being specialist places for people to enact curses. The curses at Bath were deposited into the natural hot water spring in the place now known as the 'King's Bath' from a special enclosed gallery with windows. Uley was a rural temple site on a

The King's Bath at the Roman Baths, Bath. This area is where many curses were deposited. (M. Evison, CC BY 2.0)

The Great Bath at the Temple of Sulis-Minerva, Roman Baths, Bath. (Szilas, CC BY-SA 4.0)

hillside which had several buildings in a complex together. Not all curses come from these two sites though, a scattering of others are known from elsewhere in Britain. What is interesting about the other places is that, where we can identify it, the context of the cursing is interesting. At Caistor St Edmund a curse by Vroc...sius (their full name is fragmentary) was found in the River Tas. The curse was for a group of stolen objects including bracelets, a cap, a mirror, ten pewter vessels, and other clothing that might have been taken during a domestic robbery. Others have been found in places associated with water, like the Hamble Estuary, and a drain of an amphitheatre in London. The curse from Clothall was found in a grave. These contexts tell us that there was a certain kind of place where cursing magic was supposed to happen. The link between them all is that these are dark, underworld, or otherwise hidden places – curses disappeared into flowing water or the sacred spring and could be associated with places of death like a grave or the amphitheatre. This was all an important part of the process and was linked to some of the physical alterations made to curses. Docilianus hammered a nail into his curse tablet, which was an act of aggression rather than a method of displaying it anywhere. In some curses the location of the nail was precisely placed so that it pierced the written name of the person being cursed. The name of the cursed person wasn't always known, but driving a nail through the curse added to its destructive magical properties. In the shrine of Magna Mater in Mainz (DE) curses were placed on a ritual fire, damaging or destroying them in a different way in the hope that some of this suffering was passed on to the person being cursed.

Right: A lead curse tablet from the Temple of Sulis-Minerva in Bath, Somerset. (Mike Peel, CC BY-SA 4.0)

Below: Metal detector finds of readable curse tablets remain unusual finds and might hint at undiscovered cursing places. In 2023, this fragment was discovered near Swindon, Wiltshire. PAS: WILT-534150. (Salisbury and South Wiltshire Museum, CC BY 2.0)

6

Teething Problems

Ancient sources reference teeth used as amulets to protect infants from the pain of teething. When faced with an angry or upset, red-faced, uncomfortable child with limited methods of soothing this pain, the ancient options included using this specific sort of amulet. In the first century AD Pliny the Elder, in Book 28 of *Historia Naturalis* ('The Natural History'), wrote of a series of medicinal cures for teething: 'For infants there is nothing more useful than butter ... for soreness of the gums and ulcers in the mouth. A wolf's tooth, attached to the body ... acts as a preservative against the maladies attendant upon dentition.' A later cure by Serenus Sammonicus in *Liber Medicinalis* ('The Medical Book') reads: '[Nature] afflicts us with torture when she arms us with snow-white teeth, so bind round your child's neck a horse's teeth.' Whilst these are given here as medicinal cures, I argue that the function of these was magical. Earlier I explained the concept of *similia similibus curantur* ('like cures like') and this again applies to this sort of amulet. In this case, the logic suggests that a tooth removed from an animal and worn by a human child who is suffering from teething pains has that pain reduced or removed. We'll return to this idea.

Infants and Teething

Teething has been described as the first major step in early childhood and is an indicator of the start of a change from immediate dependency on an adult to increasing levels of independence (in terms of food sources). It is a step further along the life course, but a change that comes with pain and suffering. Teething pain is natural and, if it occurs, unavoidable. Not every child suffers teething pain equally, there is a spectrum from no pain to intense pain and this might also change depending on the age of the child and which tooth is causing the problems. Studies of modern Western populations show that teething really is a variable process. It begins between four and twelve months of age, although some babies can be born with their first teeth. What this suggests is that an amulet that protects against teething pain might have had a long lifespan for a single child as well as there not being a specific age or type of child who needed one. As an aside, the medical

Sculptural detail on the sarcophagus of Marcus Cornelius Statius showing a seated mother breastfeeding her infant son whilst the father looks on. In the Louvre. (Marie-Lan Nguyen, CC BY 3.0)

writer Soranus in the first century AD mentioned the occurrence of teething at about the seventh month and recommended the massage of the gums for it, and the application of a piece of animal fat from which the infant could suck moisture.

Teething is closely associated with weaning, though the two processes did not necessarily happen at the same time. To gain a sense of weaning in Roman Britain, we can draw on both ancient writers and archaeological evidence. Soranus in his treatise *Gynaecology* recommended that breastfeeding continue up to eighteen to twenty-four months of age, with some solid food supplements. This suggestion is supported by archaeological evidence. An isotopic study of infants from Roman London found that the transitional phase of weaning often lasted up to three years of age within that population but that it was supported by a cereal-based diet from around six months of age. Other evidence suggests that breastfeeding mothers may also have used a specialised cereal-based diet and so have been particularly at risk of poor health and especially of anaemia (low iron levels).

Using a Pierced-tooth Pendant

There are more than forty examples of pierced-teeth pendants from Roman Britain which might have performed an amuletic function. A particular problem is that humans have been piercing animal teeth to wear since before the last Ice Age and so whilst discoveries of many could be Roman, they could also come from other periods. Few of these have been found associated with infant graves and they are often under-recorded. In one example from grave 450 at Lankhills (near Winchester) there were two pierced canine teeth of a dog or wolf in a grave of a six-to-nine-month-old infant dating to AD 390–410.

The identification of a tooth as an amulet requires one to have been drilled with a perforation, a simple hole usually through the root rather than the enamel. If an un-drilled animal tooth was worn as a pendant (for example in a pouch or after being bound with fine thread) then it is harder to make this link based on the archaeological remains alone. The true extent of this practice may thus have been much larger. The teeth were usually incisors, and most frequently of dog or wolf. Other animal species have also been recorded including bear, cow, horse, fox, and badger. Seven are from cows and one from a horse, which are grazing animals and have quite different teeth to the other carnivores in the list. Most of the teeth were either incisors or canines. These are biting teeth and so the magical thinking might connect the use of a tooth which may have caused pain when biting another creature to prevent pain in an infant who doesn't yet have that tooth fully developed. Perhaps the tooth pendant was supposed to attract the pain.

The two quotes given at the start of the chapter mention that the amulets were attached or bound to the infants in order to function. The requirement of an amulet to touch the person it was supposed to protect is a common theme in the ancient world and can be seen in many of the objects described in this book. Having it worn around the neck makes sense for an adult, who could do so without issue, but is more problematic for a child and especially for an infant of six months of age. A worn pendant would represent a considerable choking hazard, surely? Unless the hanging pendant was supposed to also work as sort of teething-toy. Motor developments at the time of teething allow infants to pick up objects and place them in their mouths and from experience any parent will know of their desire to put almost anything

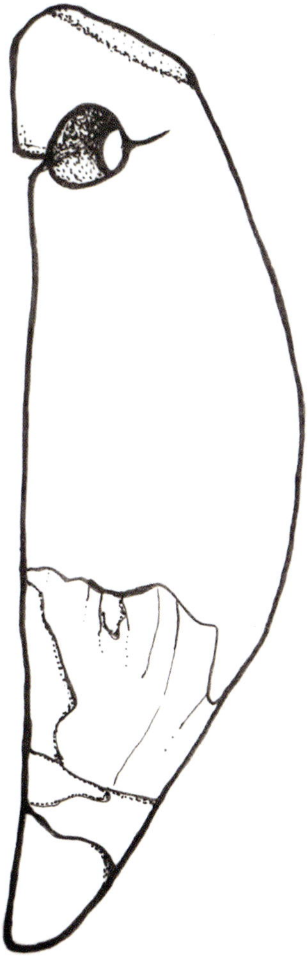

Above left: Illustration of a pierced tooth pendant from Colchester. It was fragmentary when discovered and has been reconstructed.

Above right: There are numerous references to infants being swaddled in the Roman world. Although it is earlier than the Romano-British period, this second-century BC ceramic votive shows an infant swaddled below the shoulder but still wearing a *bulla*-type necklace and offers another situation where a pierced tooth pendant could be worn by a teething infant. (Wellcome Collection, Wellcome Trust, CC BY 4.0)

they can find into their mouth to explore it. So, perhaps the amulet also had a pragmatic function? This could link with a magical one by keeping it close to the source of pain.

A tooth used successfully to get a child through a phase of teething might have been kept to work for the next one, and so gain a reputation for effectiveness. That said, there may have been specific traditions for wearing or using a pendant like this. Perhaps the sort of tooth that was expected to arrive might have been mirrored by the one being worn? Or a new tooth was required each time it became 'full' of pain? Gathering these teeth may not have been a simple thing too. Cows and horses were abundant, and dogs readily lost teeth but wolves and beavers were (in terms of pure numbers) harder to come by and unlikely to be found in urban places. Did the user have to gather teeth themselves or was there a trade in these objects? Perhaps some sorts were regarded as more effective and so were more expensive, creating an economic hierarchy of the animal teeth.

One additional thought for these pendants might be that they were, despite Pliny and Soranus's suggestions, not worn by children at all but by adults. Teething could also cause new pain in the adult breastfeeding the infant. In a tight embrace, especially during breastfeeding, a tooth pendant could be held between infant and adult and might have been used to protect both of them together.

Left: A ceramic tettina, supposedly a feeding bottle for infants. There are many variations on this vessel type in Roman Britain. From York. (© York Museums Trust, Yorkshire Museum)

Below: Pierced teeth were not as rare as the low numbers suggest, but they are difficult to find because they are organic and it is a practice that was used before and after the Roman period in Britain. This pierced tooth evidently has some age to it but we don't know when it was pierced and worn. Its colour is from the soil conditions it was buried in. From Thamesfield, London (PAS: SUR-8675FD). (Surrey County Council, CC BY 2.0)

7

Gorgoneia

The classical myth of Medusa is probably quite familiar to most modern readers. The myth is truly a success story, as it has been told on and off for over 2,500 years. Medusa was one of three Gorgon sisters. It depends on which version of the ancient myth was told, as myths changed, but usually the sisters had a divine heritage and Stheno and Euryale were immortal and their other sister Medusa was mortal. King Polydectes of Seriphus challenged the Greek hero Perseus with slaying Medusa in an effort to get Perseus out of the picture so the king could marry Perseus' mother. Perseus had the favour of the gods and was given their divine help in the form of useful tools for the task: a mirrored shield from Athena, a pair of winged sandals from Hermes, and a sword from Hephaestus. How the Gorgons were depicted artistically changed over time, from large monstrous women to the more familiar images of human-like women with snakes for hair. Medusa's gaze was able to turn people to stone, and so Perseus used the mirror shield to avoid looking at her directly and was able to decapitate the Gorgon. The decapitated head of Medusa remained alive when the hero gifted it to Athena in thanks for her assistance, after which the goddess wore it on her aegis. Throughout the Roman period, the Medusa was depicted as a disembodied head with snakes for hair. When associated with images of Minerva (the Roman version of Athena), the head can be seen on her breastplate, shield, or sometimes carried. So in images of the goddess it was associated with armour and physical defence and this is where the idea of Medusa being an amuletic image comes from. She embodied the idea of life after death, of a strong constitution, and of deflecting those who looked at her. These ideas together made images of the Medusa an amulet against the likes of the Evil Eye.

Medusa in Context

The Medusa was depicted in different media in different places, as we will explore. Unlike some amulets, like phallic imagery, there does seem to be a more restricted range of places where a Medusa may have been encountered. She is often found on floor mosaics from large villa buildings from the third and fourth centuries AD. In one from

The classical myth of Perseus and Medusa has been an enduring story for artists and sculptors since the Reformation. This mid-sixteenth-century bronze statue was cast by Benvenuto Cellini. (Dimitris Kamaras, CC BY 2.0)

Cirencester she occupies a corner of a floor mosaic, within a curving border of interlaced tiles. The central roundel in this mosaic depicts a hunting scene and the other panels contain many other natural, geometric, and probably divine images. What is important is that the Medusa isn't included in the narrative of the rest of the mosaic; she was an addition for amuletic effect. This is on display at the Corinium Museum with another Cirencester mosaic, from Dyer Street, which also includes a Medusa. The Dyer Street one is probably a more traditional use of a Medusa on a mosaic because she was placed in the centre. Her panel is smaller than the others, which included the four seasons imagined as gods and other panels with mythological scenes on them, but its location is important. There seems to have been a tradition of this arrangement – a central Medusa surrounded by the four seasons - as it can also be found on one from Brading villa and from a townhouse in York. In the four season's style, the seasons generally face two sides (so on each side two of them are next to each other and on the opposing the other two are upside down) with Medusa in the middle. In all these examples she wears a winged helmet, usually faces forwards expressionless but sometimes glancing to one side, and has two or three pairs of snakes emerging from behind her head. Floor mosaics were meant to have couches, chairs, tables, even plants on them and so often various elements of the design would have been hidden. The central position of the Medusa however, within the boundary of four seasons, is a narrative of eternal protection – within the changing year she remained ever watchful.

Copper-alloy mount with Medusa. The rounded shape of these mounts might be suggestive of a shield. From Stroud, Gloucestershire (PAS: GLO-7A3DE9). (Bristol City Council, CC BY 2.0)

Medusa depicted in the centre of the apsidal end of a floor mosaic from Dalton Parlours villa, West Yorkshire. In the Yorkshire Museum. (York Museums Trust, Yorkshire Museum, CC BY-SA 4.0)

Medusa Pendants

A small group of pendants from Roman Britain and the nearby provinces on the Continent are made from jet. Jet is a semi-precious stone and is, essentially, a form of coal formed from Jurassic-period wood under high pressure. It is lightweight, black in colour and can take a high polish. The most common uses for jet in Britain were as personal adornment such as hairpins, bracelets, and beads. Jet occurs on the coast of East Yorkshire where it was readily found by beachcombing and still can be today.

There are twelve jet pendants from Britain which depict a Medusa in the same artistic format as the mosaics – disembodied, with a winged helmet, and pairs of snakes. Four are from York, three from London, and one each from Colchester, Chelmsford, and Rochester. A tentative record of one is from Kettering. Whilst the Medusa appears on other materials, there does appear to have been a particular relationship to jet in the third and fourth centuries AD. There is a source of jet in the area of modern Germany and this was also used in the Roman period to produce pendants in the style of those found

Three jet Medusa pendants from York. Two have the front face worn smooth from where the material has been rubbed. In the Yorkshire Museum. (©York Museums Trust (Yorkshire Museum))

in Britain. Eleven further examples are known from the north-western provinces of the Empire, five of which are from Cologne. It is unclear if it is a Continental style from a different province which was imported, a British one which was exported, or something entirely different.

Returning to the importance of the material for this sort of object, there are two qualities of jet which make it particularly interesting. Firstly, because it is a form of coal (although it feels like a lightweight stone) it will burn easily. Secondly, and more importantly here, jet is electrostatic and can take a static charge. If rubbed it can attract hair and cloth fibres. This property adds a strong supernatural component to the amuletic function of these objects because it was able to do strange physical things to the world around its user if interacted with in a certain way. Now, where this gets fascinating is that there are examples of jet Medusa pendants worn almost smooth from where they have been rubbed, showing that they were used for this purpose in the ancient world.

It is interesting to find the artistic tradition of Medusa in Roman Britain, as it was wholly imported with the Roman Empire. By the time it was carved into pendants, painted on walls, or depicted in mosaic the myth was a thousand years old. There may have been an understanding of how old this tradition was in later Roman Britain and its links to deep-time and the myths and legends of (by then) already ancient places may have added to its power.

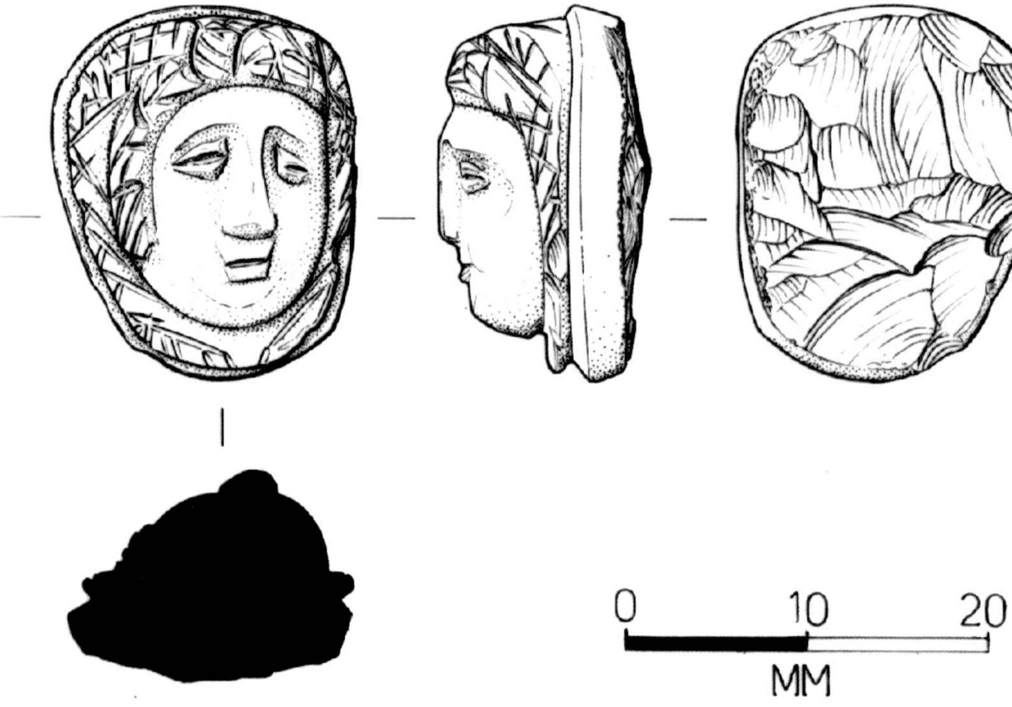

A miniature version of the Medusa face on a cameo. This was set into an item of jewellery such as a finger ring or pendant. From Breckland, Norfolk (PAS: NMS-1396BC). (Norfolk County Council, CC BY-SA 4.0)

A second-century AD mummy portrait from Roman Egypt of a woman wearing a gold necklace, a Medusa pendant, and golden earrings set with pearls. In the Kunsthistorisches Museum Vienna, Austria. (Carole Raddato, CC BY-SA)

Images of the Medusa were depicted on Roman Republican coinage and so were circulating around Britain and nearby provinces before they became part of the Empire. This *denarius* was issued by Lucius Plautius Plancus in 47 BC. From Droxford, Hampshire (PAS: HAMP2567). (Portable Antiquities Scheme, CC BY-SA 2.0)

8

Lamellae and *Bullae*

In modern scholarship these two kinds of objects are sometimes linked together. *Bullae* and *lunulae* were used as amulets and traditional interpretations draw clear gender boundaries on who wore them – *bullae* for boys and *lunulae* for girls. This chapter explores their shapes and functions as well as this gendered link.

Bullae

Bullae are small, rounded pendants. The Latin word translates as 'bubble' explaining their rounded shape, which is not unlike a modern locket. Details on their use by ancient authors, especially Plutarch (*Roman Questions*, 101) and Pliny (*Natural History*, 33.4), suggest that they were associated with high-born boys and that they were a social status symbol of this rank. Other sources indicate that the *bulla* was removed at the start of puberty and could be offered to the Lares, the family gods. So, any powerful protection offered by these amulets is not because of a link to a supernatural creature or deity or because of any magical symbols on them, but is focussed on the social associations of their shape. The traditional argument here is that high-status boys wore them and so were protected by the wealth and social benefits of class. The Roman class system was linked to its political system and elevation to a higher rank was based on meeting financial thresholds as well as some other social cues like citizenship.

On surviving statues and relief carvings in Italy there are depictions of young boys wearing such a pendant on a long string around their necks with it resting over their clothes. The statues were, inevitably, of patrician (upper class) infants and they were depicted in the formal clothing of their class. They are not common archaeological finds, but the presence of gold *bullae* does seem to indicate high status. For example, a cremation burial from Aix-en-Provence (FR) included a *bulla* in the grave goods, along with two gold rings with emerald settings and some coinage. The cremation container was made from porphyry (a rare, hard, purple stone which was prized for its colour in the ancient world). Very few surviving examples from Roman Britain can be

A marble bust of a child wearing a *bulla* amulet. From Herculaneum (IT). In the Archaeological Museum, Naples. (Public domain)

Copper-alloy figural mount depicting the Emperor Nero as a young boy, wearing a *bulla* around his neck. AD 49–60. From Drayton, Oxfordshire (PAS: SOM-EABDC5). (Portable Antiquities Scheme, CC BY 2.0)

identified and only one of these is made from gold, from Chelsham in Surrey. What is most interesting in the Romano-British objects is that where we find *bullae* they are not likely to be made of gold. Several silver examples are known and others in copper alloys. It might be logical to assume that non-metallic materials were also used which have not survived, such as leather, ceramic, even textile. A study of Romano-Egyptian funerary portraits from Fayyum by Christopher Faraone identified three examples where the person was wearing a *bulla* and all were young boys. The lived experience of Roman Britain was obviously very different from Egypt but this is a useful yardstick to use for the traditional depiction of this sort of object. The *bullae* on statues of young boys in Italy also show them worn as pendants, hung on a simple strap around the neck. These visual examples show that they were not used as parts of necklaces with other beads or amulets strung alongside them, only the *bulla*, and also that they could be worn over clothing and so were visible to other people. This was not necessarily the case for all amulets in Roman Britain.

Bullae are rare from Britain (one gold, one silver, and six in copper alloys have been identified) and *bullae* from a secure archaeological context even more so, but the few examples of this fortunate situation that can be identified tell a very interesting story: they are buried with adult women and this evidence subverts the traditional interpretation of this object. As one of these burials is definitely from the later half of the Roman period in Britain it might suggest that the role and function of this amulet changed over the course of the centuries; although it might have started as something for very young high-born boys, it's function changed and it became appropriate for women, and older women. It also highlights the use of this object as something worn in death.

The bubble-shaped amulets were hollow, but not empty. Several examples from throughout the Roman Empire have been found with their contents intact and these included plant materials (snapdragon seeds, coriander seeds, and a rose thorn) as well as more familiar magical or ritual objects (a figurine, an inscribed silver sheet with a coin,

A silver *bulla*, worn in death by the 'Ivory Bangle Lady' at York. (York Museums Trust, Yorkshire Museum, CC BY-SA 4.0)

Gold *bullae* are very rare in Roman Britain. Perhaps this is because they reached their peak popularity in the first century AD. This complete, gold *bulla* was found at Ostia, near Rome, in the very early first century. In the Vatican Museum. (Public domain)

and a small phallic amulet). The power of plants is not a topic covered in this book, but there was a great deal of ancient knowledge about the culinary, medicinal, and magical properties of plants. Just like the natural properties of stones (Chapter 11) or the inherent power of some animals (Chapter 10), plants could be used for magical purposes. The knowledge that *bullae* contained these sorts of things changes their interpretation from amulets which were powerful because of their shape and material to amulet cases which were used to carry other powerful materials.

Lunulae

Lunulae refers to objects, usually pendants, in the shape of a crescent moon. They were rigid metal pendants, unlike the hollow cases of *bullae*. Most often they were worn with the points facing downwards and a suspension loop on the back of the curving arm. Like the ancient literary sources linking *bullae* to boys, *lunulae* are particularly associated with girls and young women. In part this might be because of the moon symbol being an attribute of the goddesses Diana and Selene. Diana was the mythical twin sister of the god Apollo. She was linked to the moon and he to the sun, so they were a matching pair. Diana, also goddess of hunting, was described as a virgin and became particularly associated with girls and their protection. Selene was the goddess personification of the moon itself.

A procession on the *Ara Pacis* altar in Rome shows a young girl wearing a *lunula* as a necklace next to a younger boy wearing a *bulla*. (Miguel Hermoso Cuesta, CC BY 3.0)

The *lunula* worked as an amulet because of its symbolic link of this object to the goddess and her protection. In the ancient world there was also a link made between lunar cycles and menstrual cycles because each lasted twenty-nine to thirty days (though, of course, the latter can be much more variable). The goddess representing the moon gave her protection to women and girls because of this link. There are material links between *lunulae* and the goddess and the moon because many examples of the pendants were made from silver and so the pale grey-white colour of the material mirrored that of the moon.

There is not significant evidence from Roman Britain which links *lunulae* or *bullae* to the people that wore them; to do so we would rely on finding them in graves where the age of the skeleton could be ascertained. There is, however, an incredible series of portrait paintings of Roman people from the Fayyum in Egypt which can again be mentioned here. Mummification as a funeral rite was still popular in Roman Egypt, though it was a different process. The portraits were painted to depict the dead people and were placed upon their mummified remains. Whilst the portraits probably show an idealised version of the person, the clothing and jewellery they are shown wearing are, at least, plausible contemporary examples of the fashions. *Lunulae* and *bullae* can be seen on several different portraits and from these we can learn something about how they were worn. The interpretation of their use relies on an understanding from elsewhere in the Roman Empire but there were certainly both types of object in Britain. In the Fayyum portraits there are thirty-six *lunulae* shown and one of these is worn by a boy and the rest by adult women. There is no archaeological evidence linking this object to male-presenting people in Roman Britain, but this portrait again challenges the simple attribution of the object as only appropriate for one gender.

An unprovenanced Roman gold *lunula*. There are no gold *lunulae* from Roman Britain and this is especially fine quality with the filigree decoration. In the Walters Art Museum. (Walters Art Museum, CC BY-SA 3.0)

There are over forty examples of *lunulae* from Roman Britain, made from either copper alloy, silver, or gold. This is a conservative figure based on a rigid definition and so they were probably more common than this suggests. A spell in the 'Greek Magical Papyri' to Selene focussed on the power of women and involved writing magical symbols on a thin leaf of silver cut into a crescent, highlighting that other ways of wearing *lunulae* have not survived. It is also confusing to find that this shape of amulet was also popular on horse harnesses (not included in the number above). Mostly, the horse *lunulae* were slightly different shapes and sizes from the human-worn examples and were made from durable copper alloys rather than precious metals.

A copper-alloy harness pendant depicting a *lunula*. This is the sort of decoration expected to be found on horse harnesses and not worn by people. From Burythorpe, North Yorkshire (PAS: SWYOR-C99474). (West Yorkshire Archaeology Advisory Service, CC BY 2.0)

9

Sound and Motion

Making magic in the ancient world wasn't just about having the right materials and the right images, it could be a full sensory experience. The text on the *lamellae* was written in a formulaic way, as if it was designed to be spoken or recited at certain times. The inclusion of unusual vowel sounds and nonsensical words could also have been spoken aloud to add to the arcane nature of magical rituals. As a comparison, in English literature the classic example is the song of the witches in Shakespeare's *Macbeth*: 'Double, double, toil and trouble. Fire burn and cauldron bubble. Fillet of a fenny snake, in the cauldron boil and bake; eye of newt and toe of frog, wool of bat and tongue of dog…'. I'm not directly linking ancient magic to this sixteenth-century description of a fictional witch, but the visual imagery is evocative. The witches speak aloud in a poetic manner and recount the ingredients used in their spell and link these to the processing they are going through. The magical charms written on *lamellae* (see Chapter 4) probably didn't require a cauldron, but they do list a series of powerful figures in a specific order to help bring about their supernatural protection.

Magical Sounds

The point here is that the magical objects in the archaeological record only represent one part of a spell or ritual. In some cases they are the end point, but many other objects could have required a spoken prayer or invocation for them to be 'activated' at certain times. One specific example of this is the palindrome on the Welwyn Charm. On the front of this tiny gemstone are depicted the goddesses Isis and Bes with a lioness and a uterine symbol. They are surrounded by a Greek palindrome A[E]MEINΛE[BΛRW]ΘEPEΘWPΛBEΛENIEMEΛ (pronounced phonetically as: *ay-mean-ay-baroth-err-eth-or-abay-ay-en-ee-maya*). Like on Claudius Similis' charm, the palindrome actually has an extra letter. Trying to say this out loud, perhaps several times together, gives a strong ritual sense of the arcane. It could have been spoken whilst touching the ring to bring about the protection it intended.

Another sound used as a protective gesture in the ancient world was the act of spitting. A gemstone from the recent excavations at Bloomberg in London depicts the goddess

The image of Nemesis spitting on her chest was circulate on some Hadrianic coins. This *deniarius* was issued in AD 136. From Holme St Cuthbert, Cumbria (PAS: LANCUM-3B51FE). (Portable Antiquities Scheme, CC BY 2.0)

Nemesis pulling at the neck of her clothing to spit on her breast – this was a protective gesture. The image was also used on the reverse (back) of some coins issued by the Emperor Hadrian in AD 130–38. It is an unusual religious scene to have been portrayed in any medium, but for its meaning to have been understood it must have made sense to the viewer as a recognisable gestural act.

Bells

Perhaps the most commonly encountered magical sound was the tinkling of bells. The idea that the sound of metal reverberation was magical is a complex thing to unpick. In Christopher Faraone's *Transformation of Greek Amulets in Roman Imperial Times* he devotes a section to this phenomenon and highlights that it was a continuous idea throughout the ancient world with roots many centuries older than the Roman period. In ancient Mesopotamia for example, striking copper alloy with iron was 'thought to frighten away demons and ghosts', and this idea pervades the vast stretches of time afterwards up to and including the Roman period.

Bells came in several forms. Mostly they were small (between 3cm and 10cm in height) and almost always made of copper alloy. They could be conical, rectangular, or dome-shaped and there are a lot of variants within these types. Very often the clapper inside was made of iron, though these rarely survive as well as the copper bodies. Mostly bells were found

A classic Romano-British quadrangular bell, with its square-shaped opening and the body tapering towards its apex, which has a large suspension loop. From Crawley, Hampshire (PAS: HAMP-ADCEE3). (Winchester Museums Service, CC BY-SA 4.0)

Another common type of Romano-British bell was smaller than the quadrangular bell. This small, domed bell has iron staining on its interior from where the iron clapper has corroded. From Boddington, Gloucestershire (PAS: GLO-5D7CF1). (Bristol City Council, CC BY 2.0)

as individual objects, but the variety in their shapes suggests different functions. Smaller dome-shaped bells might have been attached to harness straps and worn by horses or other beasts of burden. The largest bells, tulip-shaped ones, could have functioned easily as hand-bells. They have also been suggested as something attached around the necks of the largest animals – cows or oxen because of their robust size. The common bells with a square or rectangular foot are more likely to have been used in many different situations, both inside and outside of buildings as well as by human hands and whilst attached to other things.

The largest group of probably magical bells from Roman Britain are a group of fifteen near-identical ones found at Coggeshall (Essex). They were deposited in the ground in a circle and all were new or nearly new when they were buried. This group was probably only rung a few times, or perhaps only once when it was buried together. The exact reason for doing so is lost to us, but it was clearly an intentional act and is probably the lasting remains of an ancient spell.

A bell was re-used as the container to deposit a coin hoard at Binnington Carr. It is one of the larger types of bell and the hoard it contained was twelve silver *denarii* dating from the first century AD. Coins were not habitually stored in strange containers like this, so something unusual is going on with this hoard. Like with most coin hoards, we do not know what the motivation for depositing it was, and especially whether it was a temporary solution where the owner was intending to retrieve them one day, or something with a ritual intent in which the coins were a dedication or payment to a deity or supernatural force.

Silver coins were found inside this copper-alloy bell from Binnington Carr, North Yorkshire. (York Museums Trust, Yorkshire Museum, CC BY-SA 4.0)

Wind Chimes

Tintinnabula, the phallic windchimes, were mentioned earlier but it is important to consider them here as well because the bells attached to the fantastical figurines are all too easily forgotten. As a reminder, a *tintinnabulum* was a windchime which usually had a phallic, copper-alloy figurine hanging from a single chain. A series of other chains hung from the figurine, each ending in a copper-alloy bell. There were usually at least three chains ending in bells, but sometimes as many as six or seven. There is only one possible *tintinnabulum* from Roman Britain, at Colchester. Its provenance at the site is a bit confused thanks to the notes left by the antiquarian collector who donated it. Most Continental examples date from around the first century AD so there is no reason that others won't turn up from Roman Britain.

In the surviving examples from other provinces, the bells are the same size rather than a group of different sizes. In modern wind chimes, the tubes or bells making the

Phallic windchimes called *tintinnabula* were designed to be visually shocking to the gaze of the Evil Eye. Many of the surviving examples were discovered in Pompeii. In the Museo Archaeologico, Naples. (Saiko, CC BY-SA 3.0)

No two windchimes were the same. They were a fantastical group of strange images and had broad appeal. It would not be surprising if similar examples are found in Britain in the coming years. In the Wellcome Collection. (Wellcome Collection, CC BY 4.0)

noise are usually set at different pitches so the sound is variable. The bells being the same size has implications for the sound the object made. If all bells were the same size, and so presumably the same tone, the sound is a repeated series of the same note – so a louder jingling, perhaps more like sleighbells than windchimes. Given the apotropaic nature of the figurines, we can presume that there was also a role for sound in these objects for chasing away the Evil Eye. To make the sound, the bells had to move or be moved and we should think about that. We don't know exactly where *tintinnabula* were used. If they were in a house, by a window then they might have been moved from the wind. Even more so if outside in a garden or hung up in a taverna (outside shop). There is also a question of whether they were handled. Being actively brushed by a hand or passively left alone could each have implications for how the amuletic effect of these fascinating objects functioned. They were a full sensory experience: bright copper-coloured objects in unusual, striking shapes, moving chaotically in the wind, and making a single noise.

Gestures

Some amuletic gestures have already been mentioned – spitting on the chest and the *manus fica* sign – but there were other amuletic gestures and acts which are hard to trace. One example is the tying and untying of knots. Publicly tying knots could be seen as a social taboo in the Roman world and even acts like crossing legs or interlacing fingers might be misconstrued as a dangerous symbol. Tying was not always a dangerous thing. The ancient names for some amulets is *ligaturae* (think 'ligature') and refers to the act of tying a spell or amulet onto someone for their protection. A Hercules Knot (what you might know as a reef knot or square knot) was also a symbol of prosperity and sometimes used as an amulet in the ancient world. A knot tied around the waist of a bride in some Roman weddings was tied using this knot and could only be untied by

A seal box lid with a stylised phallic decoration. This added amuletic protection to the physical protection of the seal. From Walsingham, Norfolk (PAS: NMS-98B5BE7). (Norfolk County Council, CC BY-SA)

A complete seal box. The interior contains holes, through which the cord is passed and into which wax is poured. The hinged lid then closes on the sealed wax, protecting it and showing the pattern of the lid. From Carnforth, Lancashire (PAS: LANCUM-422083). (Portable Antiquities Scheme, CC BY 2.0)

her spouse. An object called a seal box could be used to protect important documents or containers. They were tied with cord, this passed through the holes in a seal box and then wax covered the cord. A seal was pressed into the wax showing the authenticity of its owner. If the wax was broken then the container had been tampered with. Some seal boxes also had amulets like the phallus or *lunula* on their lids to add magical power to their physical protection.

Exactly how amuletic it may have been is debatable, but gestures which suggest bodily functions can also be found. A squatting male figure, nude except for the Phyrygian cap he was wearing, can be found atop a carving of the Evil Eye. The carving is now in Woburn Abbey but has a likely provenance of the central Mediterranean area. It's on a carving showing an all-suffering Eye (see Chapter 1) and so in an artistic tradition which could be found across the Roman Empire. A much smaller, cruder version of the squatting male figure is known from a jet plaque from Gloucester. In it, he is facing towards the viewer, very much like the *Baubo* figurines, with legs splayed apart. He might be holding a horn or something similar to his mouth, but the plaque is fragmented. Both squatting figures were probably defecating.

Broader evidence for the existence of these sorts of practices does not survive archaeologically, but their presence in Roman Britain is likely. Undoubtedly there were other protective gestures which have been lost to history.

The Evil Eye is surrounded by its enemies on this detailed marble carving. It is unprovenanced but now in the collection of Woburn Abbey. (Image from F. T. Elworthy, *The Evil Eye*, 1895)

A squatting figure carved on a jet plaque from Gloucestershire is probably showing someone defecating. It is similar in style to the figure atop the Evil Eye carving in Woburn Abbey.

10

Animal Power

In an earlier chapter, pierced animal teeth were introduced as amulets against the pain and suffering of teething. They were thought to work because of a belief in the latent power of natural objects and their magical links to certain qualities. In that chapter it was suggested that the biting teeth of some canines were used as a pendant because of an inversion of this idea – taking a pain-causing tooth out of its normal context and repurposing it to help stop pain. There are many complex relationships like this one to be found in the material culture of magic in Roman Britain where the qualities of animals could be used for the protection and curing of humans.

By way of a further introduction, we can return to the concept of the 'all-suffering Eye' explored in Chapter 1. In the depictions of this scene from across the Roman Empire the Evil Eye was being kept at bay by a series of powerful images, weapons, and animals. The phallus featured prominently, and various sharp-edged weapons make an obvious kind of sense. Commonly featured animals in these scenes, though, were mundane rather than supernatural creatures – a dog, a snake, a scorpion and/or crab, a raven, a lion. Dogs were companion animals and well known as protectors of people and spaces. A famous mosaic from the entrance of a building in Pompeii depicted a dog on a chain alongside the inscription CAVE CANEM ('beware of the dog'). This might have been a literal warning against a real-life dog, or a metaphysical warning against the idea of a dog and so a different sort of protection. Dogs were also closely linked to healing practices in Britain and were used as an avatar of the healing god Asclepius. Snakes and scorpions were known to be sneaky, Underworld creatures who were capable of causing real pain and so were probably used in this amuletic scene as sorts of living weapons. Snakes were also images of healing, and their magical nature will be explored shortly. Lions and ravens are more difficult to link to protection of people other than through being well-known animals, one intelligent and the other fierce. Perhaps these properties were useful in defeating the Evil Eye.

Snake Imagery

Identifying snake imagery on objects, mostly jewellery, as apotropaic is complicated and relies upon linking it to many different examples in magic and religion. There are three snake-like figures commonly either depicted or named on magical gemstones and other spells from the Roman world: Chnoubis, Abraxas, and Ouroboros. Chnoubis was a lion-headed snake who wore a radiating crown and its use was closely linked to curing stomach complaints. Abraxas was a cockerel-headed man with snake legs and a solar god who probably linked day and night cycles because of the cockerel representing daylight and the snakes representing darkness. Ouroboros was a snake eating its own tail and so a symbol of eternity and continuity; an Ouroboros was surrounding the other magical symbols on the Welwyn Charm (Chapter 3).

There are links to other supernatural powers as well. Snakes are linked to the Romano-Egyptian deities Isis and Serapis and to classical gods like the messenger god Mercury who held a *caduceus* (a short staff wound with a snake) and the Lares and other household deities depicted on shrines in Pompeii as snakes. A god who might be less familiar is Sabazios who is best known from their Hand of Sabazios figurines which show a human hand with fingers and thumb raised and covered in various symbols including a pinecone, human figures, scales, a ram, and a snake wound around the wrist and back of the hand. Finally, we cannot ignore the importance of snakes in the depiction of the Medusa and on *gorgoneia* amulets in Roman Britain (see Chapter 7).

There are more than 450 objects from Roman Britain which depict a snake on them. The vast majority were bracelets and finger rings made from copper alloy or silver. There were two different sorts of depictions of snakes: realistic and abstract. The realistic representations included a visibly snake-like head. The 'bodies', by which I mean the ring or the bracelet, could also have scales marked on them. Interestingly, the majority of realistic snake jewellery included two heads – in a bracelet they were slightly apart and had two

Although not from Roman Britain, this gold bracelet depicting a coiled snake is a well-attested form throughout the Empire. Note an example on the wrist of the woman in the mummy portrait overleaf. In the Metropolitan Museum of Art. (Public domain)

A mummy portrait of a woman. In addition to earrings and a necklace with a *lunula* pendant she is wearing a coiled snake bracelet around her right hand. (Public domain)

heads facing each other. In finger rings the silver heads were coiled nearby to each other. Some snake rings were very realistic and used coils to wrap around a finger.

The more realistic representations include the bony head and jaw shape of a snake. This is argued by some modern scholars to represent an Aesculapian snake. In the ancient myth, Asclepius (a god of healing) has a staff with a snake wound around it. In modern biology this snake is sometimes identified as *Zamenis longissimus*, a non-venomous snake native to much of Europe. A few, rare snake bracelets have been found in gold. These are the most realistic of the snake forms and include the zig-zagging movement of the snake, perhaps comparable to *Zamenis*.

A popular artistic alternative was the 'stylised snake' where the idea of a snake is taken and deconstructed to create a more simplistic but still recognisable form. Mostly these were made from copper alloys and the snake was depicted by a ring-and-dot eye and a few incised lines, occasionally with some scales. Snakes represented something otherworldly and like many other amulets could be interpreted in different ways. Real snakes could be

Right: A double-headed snake ring in silver. It is now bent, but both heads originally rested against the ring itself. From Ryburgh, Norfolk (PAS: NMS-7F3190). (Portable Antiquities Scheme, CC BY 2.0)

Below: Most snakes were stylised examples rather than accurate depictions. Copper-alloy bracelets were the most common form of snake jewellery. From Tuddenham, Suffolk (PAS: SF-F21177). (Suffolk County Council, CC BY 2.0)

More realistically snake-like than the other examples is this single coiled snake with the scales marked across its body. From Catterick, North Yorkshire. (York Museums Trust, CC BY-SA 4.0)

regarded as regenerative because they shed their skins occasionally and would emerge in spring from hibernation after being hidden for many months. For magical purposes they were linked to ideas of protection (through fighting the Evil Eye and on *gorgoneia*), healing (though Asclepius), and continuity (through Ouroboros and others), and these qualities were beneficial properties which the people of Roman Britain tried to bring on themselves by using snake objects.

Deer Antler Pendants

An interesting group of antler pendants, usually regarded as amulets, are found in the north-western provinces of the Empire and many of them are from Britain. These pendants were made from the base of a deer antler after it had been shed. They were cut and filed to enhance the natural rounded profile and often had imagery carved on them. Most were plain. A couple of suspension holes drilled through them allowed the pendants to be strung and worn or hung somewhere. It isn't necessarily the case that they were worn around the necks of people, but some might have been. These were chunky, prominent objects to be used as personal adornment. The flattened faces of the cut antler could have been

Found in London, the phallus carving and the four rivet holes on this antler roundel are of the second 'thinly-cut antler' type mentioned. The rivet holes show it was probably attached to something wooden rather than worn by a person (PAS: LOND-791EC5). (Portable Antiquities Scheme, CC BY 2.0)

used as a small canvas onto which other things were painted, though no evidence of this use has survived. A small group of these antler pendants included phallic images carved prominently on their surface. There were two kinds, one where the antler material was kept quite thick and used as a frame for the carving and a second where the antler was cut thinly. Usually the phallus was in a side view in low relief but at least one example (from Dorchester) had a phallus projecting from this rounded backing.

Exactly what they were supposed to do is unclear. Antler objects are sometimes thought of as hunting trophies, but naturally shed antlers could just be found at the right places at certain times of the year. The likelihood is that they were a different interpretation of the sympathetic magic links between animals and objects. Male deer are large, showy beasts and embodied some Roman qualities of virility, aggression, even security and protection in defending a harem of female deer. Stags fought and naturally shed antlers seasonally, so there were clear links to seasonality, change, and life cycles. The antler roundels could have aimed to bestow the stag qualities on their wearers or be used to protect people during times of natural change.

Bears and Big Cats

In a small number of infant graves in Roman Britain there were tiny figurines of bears or big cats carved from jet. Nine in all, there are figurines of bears in graves from York, Malton, and Colchester, and big cats (either tigers or lionesses) from Chelmsford and Chew Park (near Bristol). All are made from jet and so share the properties that made this material unusual and magical (see Chapter 11). They are also closely linked to the funerary tradition of young adult women wearing jet pendants depicting Medusa in the grave.

Bears and big cats are rare survivals in jet and have a strong archaeological relationship to infant graves in Roman Britain. This bear is from Malton. (Reproduced by kind permission of Malton Museum CIO.)

The jet Medusa tradition, as explained earlier, was quite rare and so it is interesting to find a different small tradition also happening in York and Colchester. The group of objects from Chelmsford is by far the most important for creating this link because in it a big cat figurine was found alongside a Medusa and other assorted jet jewellery. Although there were no human remains in the grave, Nina Crummy has argued that the size of the cut in the ground and the arrangement of objects suggests that it was a grave. Just like some of the Medusa pendants, two of the animal figures have been heavily worn away through rubbing. This physical interaction might have created an electrostatic charge.

The tiny figurines may have been used as toys or keepsakes (though they are very small for this) for infants, but the worn-smooth examples are unlikely to have been manipulated with enough regularity by infants to have become as worn as they are. This might suggest that the worn examples were much older than infants they were interred with, having had a long period of use beforehand. Why bears and cats? These were powerful predators. Like we saw with the pierced teeth pendants (Chapter 6), this could be a reappropriation of a dangerous animal to protect something delicate and precious. Bears were also symbols of the goddess Diana the hunter; she gave her protection to women and so these objects, relating to the tragic deaths of young infants, might be representing their mothers. One particular ancient myth is worth mentioning in this context: Callisto was a handmaiden of the goddess Diana. She was seduced by the god Zeus (who might have been disguising himself as Diana to do so) and fell pregnant, eventually giving birth to her son Arcas. Diana expelled Callisto from her service, and either Diana or Juno (the partner of Zeus) turned Callisto into a bear. In a turn of events, the son Arcas nearly shoots his mother as a bear whilst out hunting – Zeus transforms them both into stars to prevent this family tragedy. Callisto was known as the constellation *Ursa major* and her son *Ursa minor*. In the context of this myth, perhaps the tiny bear in an infant grave suggests that the mother died in childbirth, and it was an amuletic link to draw them together in the afterlife. The powerful animal acted as a sort of anchor, showing family ties.

There are other strange animals carved out of jet which survive as unique, individual objects. These include a hare from Colchester, a rod or handle with a turtlehead from York, and a handle in the shape of a dog from Binchester. Perhaps jet was particularly powerful when used for carving animals and linking it to their physical properties.

11

Uncanny Stones

Previous chapters have introduced magical objects which drew their power from their shapes, from words written upon them, and/or from how they were used. Certain materials were also regarded as important, special, or arcane. The pierced teeth pendants drew their power from a specific part of an animal, for example, and gold was important for healing spells and lead for cursing rituals. This idea, that certain materials were powerful, can also be exemplified by the use of certain 'uncanny stones'. These were naturally occurring, hard materials which could be worked into specific shapes but also possessed interesting and unusual physical properties.

Jet

More importantly amongst this class of objects in Roman Britain is jet. The properties of jet have already been discussed in Chapter 7 as well as how it was used to create *gorgoneia* and animal figurines. As a reminder, it is a form of coal, and so is black and lightweight but it takes a high polish and rubbing it can produce an electrostatic charge. Jet was a very commonly used material for female personal adornment in the third and fourth centuries AD, with a great many hair pins and necklaces beads being made from it. Were all jet objects magical, though? The evidence doesn't point in this direction, or at least it does not point towards many objects being rubbed to produce that electrostatic charge – something very unusual in the ancient world. Other relevant objects for which its strange physical properties have been used as a source of power to the object are portrait pendants. With their similar size and oval shape, portrait pendants are very similar to *gorgoneia*. They depict human figures, sometimes as individuals, sometimes as family groups, and sometimes as couples. In an example from York, a couple are posed in a formal way but looking slightly towards each other. This might have been a keepsake, or a romantic gift. In an example from Vindolanda the couple are shown to be kissing. Love charms and love magic was quite rare in Roman Britain and it is doubtful that a portrait pendant was meant to make someone fall in love with someone else. One such object, a gold ring from Corbridge, includes the Greek inscription ΠΟΛΕΜΙΟΥΦΙΛΤΡΟΝ which translates as 'the love charm of Polemius'. As noted, jet is easily found by beachcombing. It is coal and does readily burn once dried. The prominent salt on it makes the flames spit, and these qualities might have meant many jet objects were ritually burned or destroyed in this way at the end of their working lives.

Left: A couple facing each in a formal pose on this jet pendant from York probably represented some sort of love token or family memento. From York. (© York Museums Trust, Yorkshire Museum)

Below: Most jet objects were worn as beads in necklaces, bracelets on arms, or as pins in hairstyles. All jet objects might have had a magical flavour or were used for ritual purposes. A jet pin with a Cantharus vessel head from York might link to ritual worship of the god Bacchus. From York. (© York Museums Trust, Yorkshire Museum)

Jet as an unworked pebble. The smoothed, sea-rolled edge is typical of jet pieces found on the beach. This piece also shows the lamination from its earlier life as wood. (York Museums Trust, Yorkshire Museum, CC BY-SA 4.0)

Amber

Amber was not technically a stone but a form of resin, although regarded as such by ancient authors. It was much rarer than jet in Roman Britain. Amber is also an unusual colour, lightweight, electrostatic, and so is often thought of in similar terms as jet by modern scholars. Like jet, it was described as having a range of medicinal and magical properties by ancient authors. Pliny the Elder (in 'The Natural History') suggested that it might be used as a curse for fever, ear problems, poor eyesight, and stomach complaints. Most Romano-British amber came through the major Italian production site at Aquilea (Italy) from its natural source in the Balkan region. Unlike jet, most amber seems to have been imported into the Britain in the first two centuries AD, though it probably remained in circulation for long after this.

Amber was also used, primarily, for personal adornment, although it was an exotic material. Unlike jet, there is a stronger case for all amber objects to have been given a magical or medicinal function as well as a decorative one because of its rarity and its sensory properties. Most amber objects were beads and there is strong archaeological evidence to link them to a funerary function for women and children. In a study of necklace beads by Ellen Swift, around 40 per cent of all beads were in the graves of adult women and the rest in children's graves, but when only amber beads were considered, 20 per cent of these were in the graves of women and 80 per cent in the graves of children.

There are several unusual amber objects from Britain, including two figurines, a knife handle, two finger rings, three pendants, and a gaming die. There is also an unusual and unique group of images from across Britain which includes a bust of the goddess

Minerva, a ram's horn, a miniature gladiator's helmet, a mouse, a bust of an African woman, a tear-drop pendant, and a miniature fly. The animals, in particular, carved out of an exotic material can be linked to the idea of power in nature. The African bust is particularly interesting because of the group of objects it was found with (as described in the Introduction) which individually had amuletic powers, linking it to a magical use.

The physical properties of amber might have made it more likely to have been touched and handled as part of its function. It is warm to the touch, lightweight, and bright orange and could have stood out against many plain or coloured cloths. Certainly, the knife handle and the gaming die were intended to be handled in order to work, but the others could have been rubbed to try and produce another of amber's interesting qualities: a sweet, resinous smell. This undoubtedly added to its exotic allure.

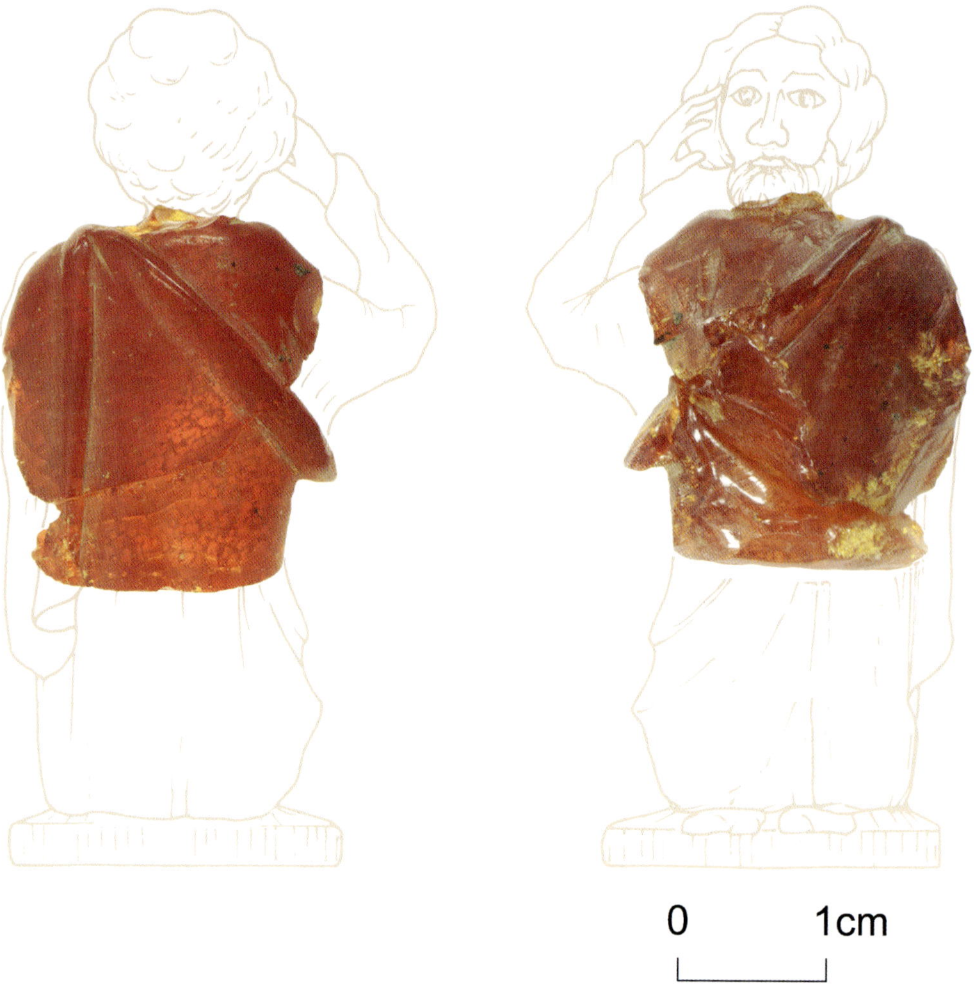

Amber was quite a rare material to find in Roman Britain, as most of it was imported from elsewhere in the Empire. It's unusual colour, texture, weight, and organic nature might have meant that it could have had a magical or ritual function in many examples. This fragment of a figure was found at Scotch Corner, North Yorkshire, and depicts a male figure in a toga. (© Ecus Ltd)

The finest amber objects are made in Aquileia and found in central Europe. Its rarity in Britain probably added to its exotic and magical nature. This character riding a cart pulled by a bird is a first- to second-century piece from Roșia Montană, Romania. (Public domain)

Fossils

Returning to British-found materials, in the same places as jet was likely to be found (and, in many other coastline places) were fossils. Many fossils have been recorded from excavations at Romano-British sites, but their ancient use is not well understood. There is a general connection between fossils and 'special' places. For example, three fossil echinoids (sea urchins) and a fossil sponge were found at Wanborough temple site, and others from temples at Titsey and Farley Heath. An ammonite was found dropped into the bottom of a well at Brislington. Several have also been found in graves. Other fossils recorded in structured deposits include *Gryphaea* (sometimes called Devil's Toenails) and Crinoids (a marine animal with a long, segmented stem and a series of feathery arms – it is the stem segments which are often found). A recent discovery in Cambridgeshire of an *Icthyosaurus* vertebra from a Roman site suggests that it was worn smooth by frequent handling. When found in the ancient world, these stones appeared as unusual, fully formed shapes already. They look organic, with natural curves and twists, and being found on the coastline meant that they were often ephemeral things, coming and going with tides, or hidden away until a chance discovery.

A Jurassic fossil bivalve called *Gryphaea*. Similar examples have been found in graves and some unusual deposits from Roman Britain. Found in Redcar. (Hallettex, CC BY-SA 4.0)

Thunderstones

Fossils were undoubtedly regarded as strange and unusual things, but they were likely to have been closely related to the places they were found. The same is true of the Roman tradition of reusing prehistoric stone axeheads as magical amulets. The axeheads are large, stone objects which mostly date from the Neolithic period in Britain. Even by the Roman period when they were rediscovered these axeheads were already ancient! Some axeheads would have been 4,000 years old by the time of their rediscovery in Roman Britain, though clearly no one would have known this information. The axeheads in question are usually the ground-and-polished types, which would appear as elongated stones with a sharp cutting edge and a tapered butt-end. They survive in many different colours and variations, although many are either red-brown or greenish in colour.

Some axeheads were associated with buildings and might have been used in roof spaces or high on walls as a deterrent against lightning strikes. This is a poorly understood tradition from the Roman period, but it certainly was a piece of folklore which survived or was rediscovered time and again throughout later British history. In more modern usage they are called 'thunderstones'. Thunderstones were supposed to be found at the sites of lightning strikes and so their re-use in buildings and other places is linked to the aphorism that 'lightning doesn't strike twice'. At least 100 examples of prehistoric axeheads have been found at Roman sites in Britain; in most cases these are single finds from a site,

Right: The Roman god Mithras was carved on one side of a Neolithic axehead repurposed as a thunderstone. He was surrounded by carved magical signs. The small stone, approximately 7cm × 5cm in size, is unprovenanced and in a private collection.

Below: This polished Neolithic axehead shows the shape, colour, and texture of this type of object. This isn't re-used as Roman thunderstone, but had it been discovered in the Roman period (like others were) it would have been an unusual, exotic thing. From near Braintree, Essex (PAS: ESS-B342ED). (Colchester and Ipswich Museums Service, CC BY 2.0)

but the baths at Canterbury and buildings at both Camerton and Fleam Dyke had several examples from one place. There is also a large group of forty-four axeheads from two ritual pits at the religious complex at Ivy Chimneys in Witham. Special deposits like this might have been intended to do something different than individual objects, which were likely to have been hung in buildings or placed in rafters. Examples from Europe include magical inscriptions and images inscribed on axeheads, linking them to other magical practices. These inscribed axes have a lot in common with the spells and magical words used on *lamellae* and gemstones in Britain.

Lithomarge

A small group of beads and objects made from a stone called 'lithomarge' have been regarded by modern authors as probable amulets. Lithomarge is, geologically, a sort of clay but has various mineral inclusions within it which cause purple and brown streaks in the stone. It is interesting in Roman Britain because its use is confined entirely to the Hadrianic frontier and Scotland. Lithomarge is most commonly worked into beads and

Unusual colours and shapes in Lithomarge make it a very 'uncanny stone'. This egg was found at Housesteads. (© Great North Museum: Hancock. From the collection of the Society of Antiquaries of Newcastle upon Tyne)

large bead-like pendants and there are at least eighteen of these in Britain. The other object type is a group of egg-shaped objects, five of which are from north of the Hadrianic frontier and a sixth from Housesteads fort on the Wall. A study by Fraser Hunter argued that the morphological differences in these eggs – that the Scottish examples were pointed, but the Housesteads egg was not – suggests a difference in their use north of the wall; that the latter was associated with Mithraism and the others a more generalised amuletic function. An 'amuletic' function is certainly ascribed to all lithomarge objects in Britain. There are no classical sources which discuss this stone, and little contextual information to back up its amuletic use, but it was clearly an exotic-looking material and exoticness and unusual materials were both often important qualities in Roman magical practices more generally.

The use of the sort of uncanny stones described here can be linked to the creation and use of magical gemstones (Chapter 3). Gemstones were, of course, also naturally occurring stones which have been adapted and used for a specific purpose. The unusual colours and shiny appearance of these stones may have helped link them to magical practices. Colour seems to have been an important feature of the magical use of stones. In gemstones, dark-red jasper was particularly used for images of Hercules and the god Mars because of visual links to blood. Black jet was used for day-to-day personal adornment but might have had a particular link to death because of an association with mourning.

12

Crepundia

By way of conclusion, let's return to the first objects mentioned in the book: a set of amulets buried with an infant in late Roman Colchester in Butt Road cemetery grave 278. The Butt Road cemetery is located outside the south-west gate of Colchester and this grave dates to Period 3 of its first phase, so in the very early fourth century AD.

The extant objects from Grave 278 at Butt Road Cemetery, Colchester. Two coins originally from the grave are now missing. (Image with permission of Colchester Museums Trust)

The objects buried with the child were a pierced tooth, a miniature phallic pendant, an amber carving depicting someone of African descent, a copper-alloy bell, two coins pierced directly, and a third held within a silver frame. These were found together with a copper chain, probably used for suspending them together as a group. This is an amulet chain, known in Latin as *crepundia*, and represents many of the different aspects of ancient magic in Roman Britain explored in the chapters of this book.

Let's first consider each of the objects here as individual things. The phallic pendant is a small example of the common amulet type, and a little unusual in its form with having a pair of raised wings at the back, but is a recognisably erect phallus. It is miniaturised to make sense in this amulet chain and was attached by a small loop on the back. It is copper alloy and so was originally the bright and brassy colour of that metal. So too was the bell. This is a simple bell with a hemispherical body (a half-sphere) and a thin copper-alloy clapper wound through a hole in its top. The noise the bell made is likely to have been a high-pitched jingle rather than a clear-sounding bell ring and it might have sounded quite similar to the other objects on the chain when they were moved together.

The pierced tooth is a classic example of this type of amulet: a dog's canine tooth. It was not fitted with any extra materials for attaching it to the chain and was simply drilled through the enamel and then strung on either with a textile cord or a narrow metal ring. The second organic material is the amber figurine. This is a unique object amongst a wider group of strange and unusual objects. Only two other amber objects from Roman Britain show humanoid faces: the goddess Minerva on a finger ring from Carlisle and a bearded man in a toga from Scotch Corner. The female figure was probably a person of African descent. The Roman Empire was a diverse and interconnected place so this in itself is not unusual but this signifier of an identity might have been particularly meaningful for the user of the amulet set.

The group of coins is unusual because of the different mounting methods used. Two copper-alloy coins were pierced directly and strung onto the chain. The third, an *as* (a coin denomination in bronze) of the Emperor Hadrian, was wrapped in a silver frame which had a suspension loop above it. The frame has a solid back so one particular side of the coin was chosen for public display and this did not show Hadrian's profile (the 'heads' side) but the reverse ('tails') side in which Hadrian was riding a horse and using a spear to stab at a fallen enemy. By the time this coin went into the ground it was over a century old, and probably over two, so was an antique. Low-value coins of Hadrian were unlikely to still be in circulation in the third and fourth centuries and so it had been selected specifically, after having been kept or found, and suspended in this unusual way. Suspending a coin on a chain transformed it from currency to jewellery.

The objects hung on this chain were all interesting objects, like curios or keepsakes. Hung together they created a disparate collection of things which is probably familiar to modern readers as a charm bracelet. *Crepundia* are recognised as unusual groups of objects. In order to categorise them, Stefanie Martin-Kilcher defined them as including five distinct types of objects: noise-making objects, meaningful shapes, things with 'exterior qualities', remarkable objects and curiosities, and materials valued for their special properties. Whilst the modern definition of what makes *crepundia* is quite loose, there are elements of these aspects in the objects in this set from grave 278. This group is probably the best example of this from Britain but it is not alone. Other *crepundia* amulet sets have been identified.

For example, in another infant grave at Butt Road cemetery, grave 406, the infant was buried with a chain with beads made from amber, black glass, jet, and yellow glass and also included were a pierced coin and a silver *lunula* pendant. In grave 180 from Bainesse, near Catterick, a child's grave contained a small flaccid phallus pendant, three hexagonal tube beads in green glass, four spherical beads in pale-green-blue glass, and five jet beads.

One thing that appears so important to this type of object is their sensory aspects. They were a riot of colour and made of strange shapes. Glass beads moving together might have made a noise and loose metal things close together certainly did, even before the bell came into use. An association with infant children might make sense here as this sort of collection of objects could have been very stimulating or pleasing for a little one. The idea of giving babies rattling, noisy toys or things to chew and investigate to calm and engage them is quite straightforward and *crepundia* might have worked like this. What takes them into the realm of magic is the complicated collection of images and symbols, materials, and colours all together which could (as individual objects) all have functioned

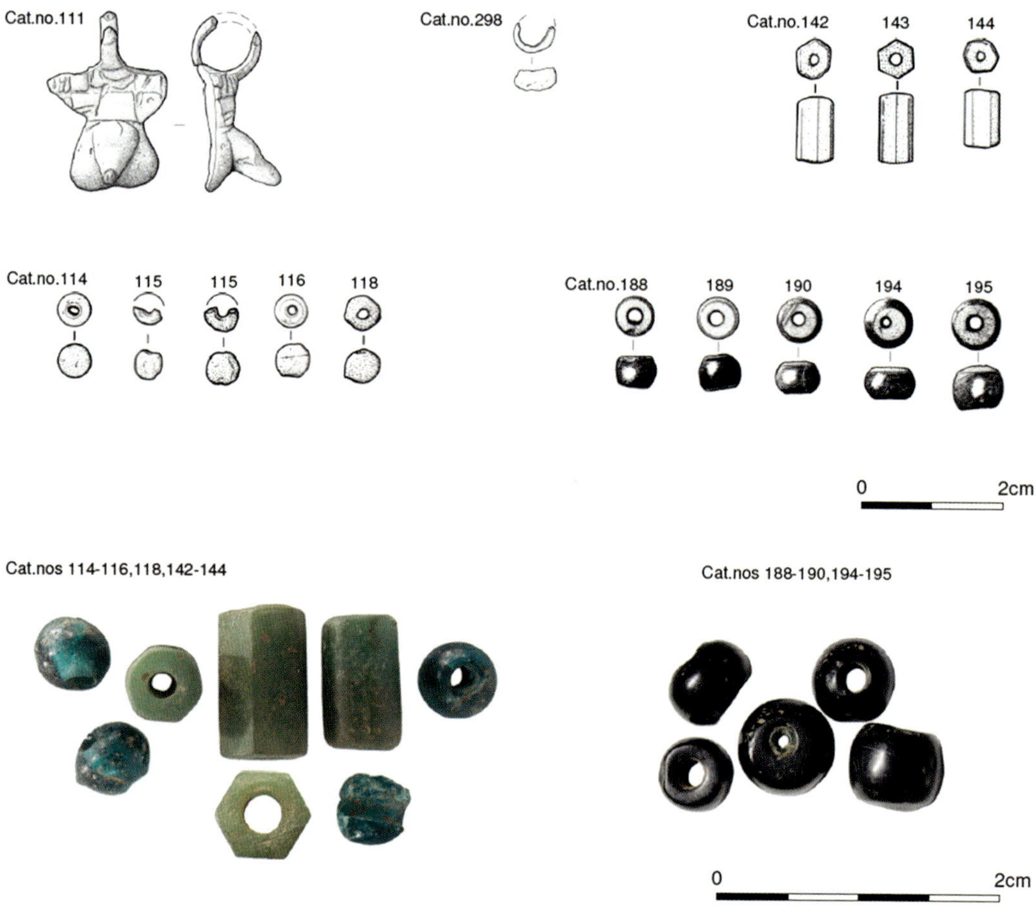

Grave 180 from Catterick, North Yorkshire, included a group of glass and jet beads alongside a flaccid phallic pendant. They were found together in a group indicating they were connected. (© Ecus Ltd)

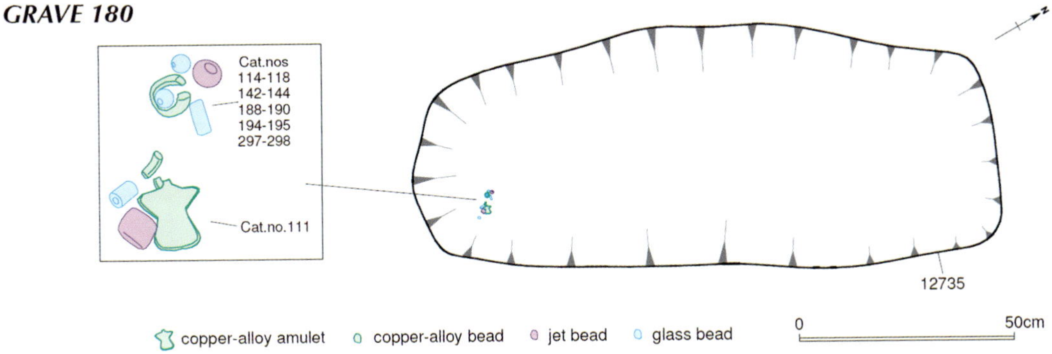

Drawings and photographs of the various elements of the *crepundia* from Grave 180 at Catterick. (© Ecus Ltd)

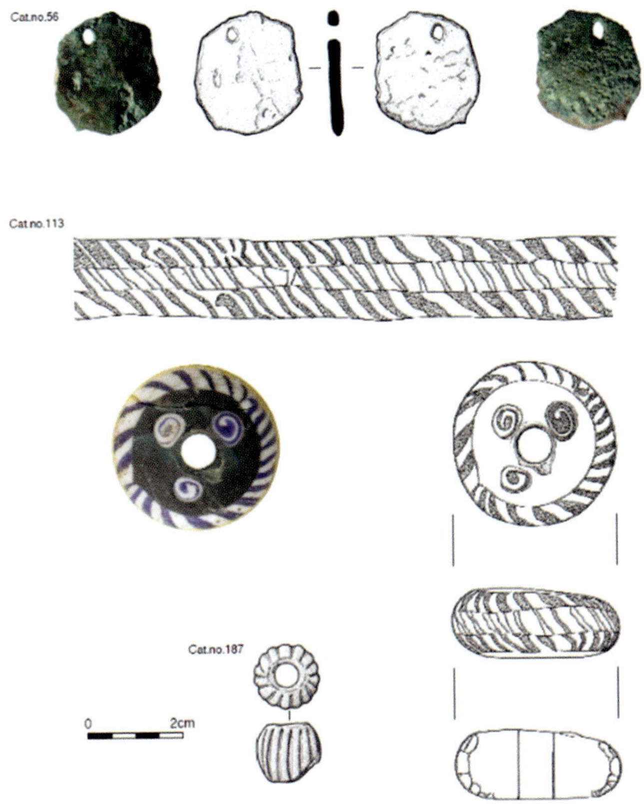

Photographs and illustrations of the Grave 221 assemblage showing another probable *crepundia* assemblage from Catterick's Bainesse cemetery. The figure omits two copper-alloy beads which fragmented irreparably during post-excavation analysis. (© Ecus Ltd)

as amulets. Most of the magical objects mentioned in this book were found as individual things – single, powerful objects doing something important for their user. So, groups of many amulets seem to be showing us something else. There are two different options for this. On one hand, the combination of different amulets together might be adding layers of power together, building up more powerful magical protection in the round to try and create an impenetrable magical shield against dangerous supernatural effects. On the other hand, each amulet could have been specifically protecting against one sort of harm like toothache or stomach problems or fevers and/or bestowing a beneficial property like strength or endurance and aimed to build up a specific defence together.

These variables are also true of most of the other magical objects presented earlier. In some cases we can suggest what harms they were trying to protect against or who they were trying to protect. In the case of curses they often tell us what harms they were trying to inflict. The context in which we find these objects is incredibly important to their understanding. This context includes both the archaeological context, where they might be associated with a grave or a building and might have other evidence which helps to date the finds, but also the social context which links certain practices to different people in Roman Britain.

This book aims to be a broad introduction to the subject, but a focus on the material culture of magic within a single Roman province highlights the complexity of this phenomenon. There are many different links between different sorts of magic, through differences or similarities in material, images, or function. Groups of magical objects like *crepundia* remind us that using magic was a targeted act and that it was often the end result of a wider process or ritual and that these were meaningful objects for the people who used them.

Further Reading

By way of a more specialist introduction to the different aspects of ancient magic, I recommend the following books:

Ager, B. K., *The Scent of Ancient Magic* (University of Michigan Press, 2022)
Betz, H. D. (ed.), *The Greek Magical Papyri in Translation* (University of Chicago Press, 1992)
Edmonds, R. G., *Drawing Down the Moon: Magic in the Greco-Roman World* (Princeton University Press, 2019)
Faraone, C., *The Transformation of Greek Amulets in Roman Imperial Times* (University of Pennsylvania Press, 2018)
Graf, F., *Magic in the Ancient World* (Harvard University Press, 1997)
Mastrocinque, A., Sanzo, J. E. and Scapini, M. (eds), *Ancient Magic: Then and Now* (Franz Steiner Verlag)
McKie, S., *Living and Cursing in the Latin West* (Bloomsbury, 2022)
Merrifield, R., *The Archaeology of Ritual and Magic* (1987)
Sánchez Natalias, C., *Sylloge of defixionies from the Roman West* (BAR Int. 3077; BAR Publishing, 2022)

These works introduce the wider topic of ancient magic and some of practices mentioned within them have not been found in Roman Britain. Note that much of the academic work of these and other authors is available for free on website repositories ResearchGate.net and Academia.edu.

Whilst one magical poppet is known from Britain and might have served a similar purpose, a clay figurine from Egypt shown to be bound and stabbed with pins was a visceral component of a cursing ritual. In the Louvre. (Marie-Lan Nguyen, CC BY 2.5)